How to Help
When Parents
GRIEVE

OTHER BOOKS BY HOLLY FOX VELLEKOOP:

~

STONE HAVEN: Murder Along The River
Avalon

How to Help
When Parents
GRIEVE

Holly Fox Vellekoop, MSN

Practical methods to help grieving parents.

Compelling stories from parents who have had
children pass away. The parents tell how they
felt and how they coped with their grief.
What people said and did that helped
and what did not.

Find grief support groups on the Resource Pages

BLUE NOTE BOOKS
F L O R I D A

Published by Blue Note Books, Florida
1-800-624-0401
www.bluenotebooks.com

www.hollyfoxvellekoop.com

Library of Congress Control Number: 2009912280

ISBN-10: 1-878398-25-3
ISBN-13: 978-1-878398-25-3

First U.S. Edition 2010

Printed in the United States of America

For Our Children

The Other Side of Heaven's Gates
By Holly Fox Vellekoop © 2009

My fingertips touch gently to sad lips.
A kiss imparted warm is blown your way.
The hand goes up as if to reach the sky
but softly bids farewell on arm a'sway.

We met, a babe and parent, new and young,
your dedication to our God confirmed.
Wings carried milestones passed, each motion made
to take you onward bound, secure, affirmed.

Dear, who alone can capture life so full
of vivid colors racing day to night?
Slow down, slow down, too quickly time has passed.
You're fading from our view, toward healing light.

Sweet smiles and laughter dim, now memories drift
'cross chasms you impart in hearts of love.
But we shall meet again, my precious one
the other side of Heaven's gates above.

DEDICATION

This book is dedicated to the parents
who have shared their stories within
these pages and to their beloved children.
Please accept my heartfelt thanks and affection
for honoring us with your tale of loss, love, grief
and faith. I am humbled by your trust.

This book is also dedicated to the nearly one
in five of the adult population who face each day
having experienced the death of a child.

A special thank you to my husband
Dr. Ronald Vellekoop and my sister,
Mrs. Fran Gilbert for their support
of my efforts in writing this book.

"Thank You" to my son Rev. Dr. Brian R. Seidel
for his love and steadfast vigilance
at his brother's bedside with us.

CONTENTS

Disclaimer

T HIS BOOK PROVIDES GENERAL INFORMATION gathered from the author's interviews with others and is meant for educational purposes and not intended as medical advice. The information is meant to inform and educate the reader but is not meant to substitute recommendations from licensed health care providers or any other care one is receiving or should be receiving. It is intended to enhance individuals' goal of optimal level of wellness but individuals should use it in cooperation with health professionals and trained practicioners. Neither the publisher nor the author is responsible or liable for any use or misuse of the information contained herein.

Introduction

WHO CAN KNOW HOW PARENTAL grief will express itself? The answer is this: Only the parent who is grieving knows; they learn it along the journey. Included within these pages are my interviews of parents who have experienced the death of a child. They recount what happened with honesty and dignity, outlining for the reader how the loss occurred, how their lives were changed and the ongoing lifelong path along which tragedy took them. Who can know what to say, what not to say, what helps and what hurts a parent who is grieving? And which of us really knows where we will be or what we will experience in our lives before we pass? So let us leave our prejudices of what "Should be done," or "What we would have done," behind. Read on and learn as did those of us who have lost a child.

The idea for this book came from my personal experience which started when my younger son Brandon first told me he had colon cancer. On the other end of the phone, I could barely breathe. Shock set in after hearing his explanation about his illness. I hung up the phone and cried, knowing he had an uphill battle. God spoke to my heart and told me, "I am calling him home." I shared this Godly message with my husband and my sister and with much prayer, eventually came to a place of trusting God with my son.

After telephoning family and friends, and placing him on every prayer list they knew existed, we prayed daily for Brandon's body to heal and for him to recover from this dreadful illness.

When Brandon passed away after a two-year battle with cancer, I experienced such a well of sadness and grief that I thought I could not claw my way out of it. I had been staying on his property in a travel trailer for the last seven weeks of his life in order to help take him to his chemotherapy appointments and other doctors' visits, and eventually help take care of him until he passed away. Brandon and I had time to talk about life, heaven and God. About his soul, his joys, and concerns in his life.

There were topics that we did not discuss due to our own personality traits and for other reasons, but I learned to accept that and to be grateful for every minute we had together. I am thankful for this time because I knew that many other parents had experienced the death of a child before they were able to say their goodbyes.

As days passed, watching Brandon's body deteriorate was more than difficult. Words cannot adequately describe my feelings as he went from ambulatory and speaking to bedfast, and then to nonverbal. His pain was managed and we appreciated the palliative care that he received from professionals. Still, bitter tears flowed and prayers continued for his healing as he lost ground. We had hoped to God that he would be the one to beat the disease.

'Please God heal him,' we asked. I envisioned him getting up off the hospital bed upon which he reclined in his living room, smiling broadly, and asking for something to eat. But it was not to be. And both he and I knew it. We had already had that conversation.

In the morning, after he died, I went into my travel trailer and, with my older son present, the two of us grieved our way, in private, over Brandon's passing.

While all along I had believed there was a good chance he would not beat the cancer, I still was not prepared for the depths of despair into which one can be thrust when the end finally comes. The visceral pain was so intense that I could not speak to the many people who stopped by at his home to offer their condolences. Words would not come. They just would not. I could not make myself walk down to his home, visit with the well-meaning people, eat with them, and share our collective grief. It seemed too much like a celebration. One for which I had no energy. I was a mother who had lost her son and I was not in a place to do any of that. My life had changed.

Because of things that were said to me, I became convinced that only parents who have lost a child could possibly know what I was going through. I wished I had something to read that would help me to understand this walk I was taking—something written by someone who had been down this road, too, so I could be sure that they understood what I was feeling.

Having read grief books in the past, I decided to revisit them. None that I read gave first person accounts of their stories of how they got there, the death of the child which began their perilous grief journey, and intimate accounts of their grief walk. I wanted to hear from others who suffer as I.

Those of us who have lost a child, even though time passes, have continuous vague feelings that something has gone terribly wrong in our world, casting a shadow on our activities and future. Those feelings abate—then resurface, causing us to feel again that something is wrong. And we wonder how to help ourselves.

I had questions about what I was feeling. Did other grieving parents feel the same way as I? What about parents whose child had passed away under other circumstances than mine, such as murder and other acts of violence, childhood disease, or a car accident? What about the parents whose child took their own life or died in a war zone or military conflict or setting? And how about those whose child passed away in utero before being born, or shortly after birth? Did the circumstances of the child's death make a difference in how the parents grieved, the form it took, and the duration? How did they feel? What helped them?

After my son passed, because of those thoughts and feelings, I decided to interview other parents who had lost a child, document their personal tales, and present them for all of us to learn something. That is some of what you will find within the pages of this book.

Intended for a broad audience, there is the hope that through our stories there will grow an understanding of what we grieving parents endure. We desire that many will find the help needed to mend their broken hearts. Perhaps readers will learn and be guided by actions and words that help the grieving parents, and avoid those that only offend or cause more harm. Pastors, health-care workers, those who interact with the dying and their families, can all glean nuggets of wisdom from those who have gone before.

Interviewing parents about their deceased child begat a series of stories within this story, each one precious and complete in itself. They are told with the utmost respect and honor for each family and child, without judgment or prejudice. I wish for it to remain so, for who can know what is the right or wrong way to grieve for another? Who can know what we will do if, God forbid, we lose a child? It is unknowable.

As a grieving parent, I found myself affected by the intensity of emotion and loss embedded in each story shared. Often, the parents cried. When they cried, I did, too and they allowed it without discomfort. We cried for their loss, for mine, and for those who have buried a child.

Through these anecdotes, I discovered how the life of every child the grieving parents shared, is layered with stories of schooling, friendships, work histories, family and community. They percolate with feelings such as love, happiness, disappointments, appreciation and gratitude. They resonate with the "what could have been"—graduations unattended, missed proms, nonexistent marriages and offspring, and most of all, their future. All of these potential life milestones, gone with the last breath of our beloved sons and daughters, affect parental grief.

But we are not without hope. The hope of seeing our child again in heaven is at the top of the list. Many believe that, when it is our time to cross over, our precious child will be among the first to greet us and we look forward to that day, whenever it shall come. There is hope that we will heal with God's help and the help of family and friends. There is hope that we can help another who suffers as we do. There is hope that we will face each day with our loss, and get through it as we did the day before.

The reader should understand that some of the content of this book was driven by side conversations with interviewees that were not recorded in their entirety within. The honesty and purity of the testimony was touching. All of the difficult personal details of their family lives were offered as a gift of help to those of you who are reading this now. So read on with an open mind and a grateful heart.

CHAPTER ONE

Grieving

TO BETTER UNDERSTAND GRIEF and how to help those who grieve, it is important that we listen to the ones who have experienced it. Through their stories, such as the ones in this book, let them speak to your heart about how grief manifested itself to them.

We read differing time frames for how long parents should be expected to grieve. In addition, friends and family have their expectations and are sometimes puzzled when the grieving don't live up to them. Experience and expectations do not always have the answers.

What we learned from parents interviewed for this book is that no matter how long it has been, there is still a measure of grieving present in their lives. "We get through each day," one said. "But we are never the same. Our lives are never the same." Another said, "I think of my child every single day."

7

We learn from history that while there are shared experiences in grieving, many have not dealt conventionally with it. In fact, some people do things that could be considered to be out of the norm. President Lincoln and his wife Mary are two famous historical figures who come to mind. They experienced the deaths of two sons before Lincoln was assassinated, and Mary suffered the loss of yet another son who passed away six years after his father was buried.

Edward Baker Lincoln, born March 10, 1846, passed away February 1, 1850, at the age of almost four years old. One theory is that he died from tuberculosis. His mother, Mary Todd Lincoln, initially was unable to go through his clothes in his bureau but finally did so and gave his clothes away to another to use.

The Lincolns' son, William "Willie" Wallace Lincoln, born December 21, 1850, was 11 years old when he passed away on February 20, 1862, possibly from typhoid fever. Mary was so upset by his death that she could not attend his funeral. After Willie was interred in a crypt, it is documented that his father, Abraham Lincoln, returned back to the crypt on two separate occasions to where Willie's body lay. Deeply saddened, on both occasions, Lincoln lifted the coffin lid to gaze upon his precious son. How that grief-driven act would be interpreted by today's press and presidential detractors is anybody's guess.

Years later, after President Lincoln was assassinated, Mary endured alone the death from tuberculosis of their son Thomas "Tad" Lincoln, who was born April 4, 1853, and died on July 15, 1871, at the age of 18.

Mary came to believe that she had bad luck in her life.

The Lincolns are not the only well-known family to have suffered grievously from the loss of one or more children. Mark Twain suffered the tragic deaths of three of his beloved four children.

His first child Langdon was born on November 7, 1870 and died at the age of 22 months from the effects of exposure to the cold. Twain blamed himself as the cause of the child's illness and passing. He had taken the child on a ride in an open carriage for some fresh air. At some time during the long ride, the fur wraps fell from around Langdon, exposing him to the cold. By the time Twain noticed it, it is reported that the child was almost frozen. He rewrapped Langdon, but the child was already harmed. Imagine the horror and guilt that Twain felt. He wrote about the shame he felt for his part in his child's condition.

For any parent to believe they had a part in the child's death, there must certainly be additional burdens and sorrows.

Twain's second child, daughter Susy, was born March 19, 1872, and died August 18, 1896, from meningitis at the age of 24. Her death was another terrible blow to him. Those of us who have lost a child can understand the horror of not only one child passing, but then another. But there was more heartache in Twain's future.

The Twains' third child, daughter Jean, died on December 24, 1909, from a convulsion and heart failure. Upon her death, Twain reminisced about the deaths of his previous children and his beloved wife, many years before. His surviving daughter Clara had moved abroad and Twain felt quite alone.

Due to his immense grief, Twain felt unable to attend Jean's funeral. He believed he was unable to endure another burial of one of his children.

It was interesting to note that some of the parents I interviewed could not attend the funeral, wake, memorial or meal after the service, too. Some expressed that it was because they were sad or because it seemed to be too much of a "party or celebratory atmosphere" when they did not feel like celebrating. Conversely, some interviewees found the services and the company of others comforting, so they attended.

We can learn from the grief experiences of parents such as the Lincolns and the Twains. Grieving that one may consider to be inappropriate or bizarre, others may find to be ordinary or even necessary in order to cope. If the actions are not harming one's self or another, who is to say what is right or wrong? Again, only those who experience the grieving can know.

One of those I interviewed said to me, "The world is allowed to grieve indefinitely for Elvis, but we parents are not allowed to grieve for our children." There is truth in that statement about the judgments that societies and individuals make about the way parents express their grief. Available on a daily basis are advice and criticisms given by some who do not face this daily struggle or by others who believe they know a formula for successful grieving.

Should the grieving parent involve themselves in busy activities to refocus attention to that which does not include their sorrow? Or should they face grief head-on and open up and expose the pain-filled spot that's buried deep within their core in order to help it heal? Or is there yet another way or ways for the grief-stricken to follow?

If refocusing on something other than the loss of a child assists one to deal with the grief, and it is not harmful, then that is right for them. This is something each must answer alone. None other can do it for them.

Some may try to advise or even accuse the grieving parents in an attempt to press their particular view on the grieving person. While doing that may be hard for the well-meaning to resist, those interviewed suggested that people not do that. Again, only the parents know what must be done to relieve their pain. Sometimes, they struggle to find something that helps. Other times, interventions by friends and family assist them to cope.

For these situations, one size does not fit all. One treatment is not to be prescribed as a blanket remedy for everyone even if it is something that worked for you. That does not mean it will be successful for another. Others' imagined grief response may be what they believe they would do should the horror of losing a child happen to them. The reality may be something entirely different. Because of the uniqueness of the loss and the events surrounding it, grieving parents are entitled to express their sorrow in a manner that works for them.

There are some practical measures that grieving parents can take to assist in easing their grief. When able to do so, refocusing on an activity or cause of interest other than the child's death is helpful. It may be impossible to do that for awhile after the death but, at some point, it should be attempted and encouraged.

When one can shift one's attention to something other than the child's death, even if only for a short while, relief from the sadness may take place. Two of the interviewees in this book assisted in crafting and pitching legislation to make it illegal for anyone to ride in the back of a pickup truck as their son was killed when he fell out the back during an accident. Parents of Junny Rios-Martinez fought for and successfully passed the Junny Rios-Martinez Act of 1992 which dealt with the early release of sex offenders from prison. Other parents have reported success with refocusing from the death of their child and the issues surrounding it to the happier times that they shared together in life. Still others, when thoughts of their deceased child arise, suppress them, purposely pushing them from their minds, claiming that brings them the much-needed relief they seek. Some of the grieving tried more than one way to relieve their pain, depending on how they were feeling that day.

After talking with many parents who had lost a child, I realized that, in many ways, my own personal grieving experience paralleled theirs. Many of the parents whom I interviewed shared similar responses to losing their child. Responses like the feeling of falling into a pit or a well from which they could not seem to get out. The words disbelief, anger, shock, feeling guilty, and denial were used by them to describe their response.

There seemed to be no universal order for the feelings to present themselves. For one it was first denial, for another their first emotion was anger. Almost all of them reported crying, some hysterically, screaming over and over. A few became stoic for the sake of others or went back to work so they wouldn't have to think about it. Work necessarily diverted their attention from their loss to the job at hand. There were others who could not go back to work because of the questions from fellow workers. Many reported they initially found themselves in shock and/or feeling numb. Depression with accompanying disinterest or inability to take care of self plagued some interviewees. There were a couple of people who blamed God or yelled at him, but I was struck by how infrequently that was mentioned.

There were even those who confessed to feelings of wanting to kill themselves because of their grief. Some admitted they made suicide attempts. Thankfully, they were unsuccessful. Those cases underscore the importance of having someone with whom to talk and the need to seek professional help immediately should suicidal thoughts occur.

Recognizing that there were accompanying issues experienced by the parents in the death of each child gave the responses more clarity. One of the interviewees,

Keith, had lost his legs in a tragic accident prior to his daughter's passing. So, he and his wife were dealing with all that was brought to their family in addition to their child's illness and death. Dwayne had lost his job around the same time his daughter passed, which added more pressure for him and his family. Lee had a prescribed tubal ligation after her miscarriage, which meant she would not experience the large family that she had hoped for and dreamed of all her life. Doris W., whose son died, had to pack up and move her family to another town shortly after he passed because her husband was transferred to another job. The move added more stress for them. All of these extra difficulties and problems that the families experienced only added to their struggle with their grief. Alone, any of these life-changing stressors would be cause for emotional trauma. Add the death of a child to the mix and it is easy to see why many of those interviewed were depressed and had long-term sadness. Life dealt these parents more than one terrible blow and then they were expected to go on living and dealing with its normalcy.

The feelings and grief of other family members and friends may also compound the parental sorrow. Siblings, extended family and friends of the deceased child mourn, too, and sometimes the parents have to deal with that. They may be at different stages of coping with the loss and want to either talk about it or not talk about it, which could be in direct opposition to where the parents are. And they may want to stop by and spend more time at the home of the parents than the parents can tolerate. Not everyone wants people grieving with them. Some prefer just very short visits or none at all. Grieving parents should be free to make those needs known without criticism from others.

I give a nod here to grieving stepparents who are often marginalized or forgotten, only to suffer alone in their own sadness and grief. They are often pushed to the sidelines and left to grieve in solitary. Stepparents love the stepchildren, too, and their grief needs to be validated for them to recover. Besides loving the child, stepparents love the natural father or mother of the child and suffer for what their spouse and other family members are enduring.

The grieving travel their grief road, moving forward through stages and changes of emotions. They can never return back to some special moment that was shared with their beloved child, except in memories.

We who grieve walk on with both the good and the bad in our lives, trying to make sense of our loss while burdened with the feelings engendered. That is important to acknowledge because those of us left behind can hopefully use our grief to make better decisions for our present interactions with loved ones.

Grieving parents necessarily manage to enter back into their work, community and family lives. They go about their activities of daily living with the level of enthusiasm and energy of which they are capable. It is interesting to note that many of us report that what you see on the outside, though, is not what is really going on in our hearts. Yes, we participate as we must, reacting to others appropriately, but a measure of sadness and awareness of our loss dwells just out of reach, within our core.

All of the interviewed parents testified to recalling their loved one on a daily basis, sometimes with laughter and sometimes with grief-tinged tears. Memories and grief were triggered just by getting awake in the morning, seeing photographs or mementos, or an occurrence in their daily routine. Sometimes the tears came for no specific reason.

In their grief, some parents leave their child's photographs out and others put them away. Anita put all of her daughter's pictures in a box along with the letters her child wrote to her. She gets them out once in awhile, spreads them on the floor, looks at the photos and reads just one letter. That makes her feel better. Then she puts them all out of sight until she feels ready to look at them again.

As for me, at first, recent photographs of Brandon made me feel sad, reminding me of his pain and suffering. So, initially, I put those photos away. Only pictures of him as a child and another as a teen standing next to his brother remained out. Both show him happy and carefree, the way that I want to remember him. Six months later, I was able to display in my office, a few recent photos.

Like other facets of grieving, there is no one way to handle the question of whether to have the child's pictures out or put them away. The methods we use and the decisions we make in this process may change as time presses on and the newness of our grief fades or we learn more coping mechanisms.

The present-day thoughts of the deceased child are different from one parent to another. Babs thinks of her daughter as being in Russia, for that is where she had been before returning home to Jamaica where she died. It helps Babs to think of her daughter as being there instead of being dead. Doris W, who lost her son when he was three, pictures him as the grown man he would have been had he lived. Most remember their loved one as they were when they passed. Regardless of how the parents think of their deceased child, they think of them daily. Sometimes it is with laughter at a fond memory of their beloved and sometimes the memories bring tears and sadness.

How we choose to remember our child is our choice and we can either do what helps us to cope, or we can torture ourselves with other thoughts—the 'what ifs,' or 'what we could have done' or 'should have done.' One must dispel those notions with the gift of forgiveness of ourselves and others so that we can go on in peace. Forgiveness frees us up to live our lives to the fullest instead of robbing us of sleep and crippling us with second-guessing and guilt. Forgiveness lifts the burden from us and also from those we forgive.

One parent expressed relief that her deceased child

had not been to the home where she presently lives. She is glad that she does not have to face the fact that her daughter lived in or visited the house wherein she must awaken each morning. Then there are Dwayne and Lisa who began adding a much-needed extension to their home, rather than moving, because they and their remaining children could not imagine leaving the house that they once shared with their deceased child. These are personal choices for the grieving.

Doris and Keith memorialized their daughter with a garden at the entrance to their home. "It's Kelly's Garden," they say. A bench for resting and thinking of their little one overlooks a fountain that relaxes the one who is contemplating Kelly. Bill and Sandy have a memorial garden, too. Each of the items within the memorial area had a special meaning to Sandy's daughter Randy. Soon, Randy's ashes will occupy the peaceful spot that her stepfather fashioned. While this has been soothing and comforting for Doris and Keith and Bill and Sandy, it is not for everyone. There are some who have added their child's ashes to their property and then regretted it because of the constant reminder when they pass the area where the ashes rest. Parents should think it through carefully, allowing some time to pass before deciding one way or another because once the ashes are spread about, they cannot be retrieved.

The important thing about how you memorialize your child is this: If it makes you happy to honor your child with something special, then by all means, do it. If you find something like that depressing, it may not be right for you and could hinder your healing. Be sure to give yourself enough time before committing to something that cannot be reversed.

Though the losses from one parent to another are different—different child, sex and age, different circumstances of passing and different family dynamics—we have a shared experience of having met the dreaded companion 'Grief.' He is with us daily, embedded deep down in our souls. We have looked in his face. We know where he lives. As time goes on we learn to survive though Grief won't leave us. We must remind each other that we will survive. And we do. However, our lives have changed and we know it will never be the same. So we must somehow learn anew how to live life without our child. Family gatherings and celebrations will be altered and new traditions must be found.

Most grieving parents also have what I call an 'Alone Grief.' This is that grief that we carry within us whenever we are by ourselves and cannot or do not want to get out to be with people. Alone Grief sometimes seems to be more powerful than when we are in the company of others. For those who know Alone Grief, it is magnified by our 'mom feelings' or our 'dad feelings,' depending on our parental role. The Alone Grief is more difficult to cope with if we don't have some plan for beating it down.

Suggestions For Relief From The Grief

❧ Prayer and scripture reading. Find the passages that speak to your soul. If you have a prayer shawl, wrap yourself in it and start thanking God for all your blessings. Ask your pastor, family and friends for verses that speak to what you are going through.

* A special book that is a real treat to read could be kept somewhere just for the times that Alone Grief appears. Read it only on these occasions and make sure it is an amusing or uplifting story or a book of your favorite genre.

* Look for an inspiring or fun-filled television show or a DVD movie and give yourself the luxury of watching it in bed. Let your spouse know ahead of time you might have to do this once in awhile and ask them to join you. Let the laughter pour forth and share it with your spouse.

* If it is a particularly hard time, have an Alone Grief friend whom you can telephone at that time who will talk with you and help you get through it. Use those times to talk about good memories you have of your child if that comforts you. Sometimes, those who have lost a child wonder if they could ever comfort another when they are unable to be comforted, but many have proven themselves to be of help and this is one way they can do that.

* Journal the feelings you are having. Reread them and share them later with someone, if that helps. Make lists in your journal of the many good times you shared with your child, your child's good qualities, things you would want to say to him or her now, then read it to your child as if they are listening.

* Practice mild exercises and/or a skill you have learned. If you enjoy gardening, step outside in the

wonder of God's creation and observe the beauty of your plantings.

❧   Listen to music that you enjoy. Let it wash over your soul to assist in your healing. In particular, listen to music that invokes happy or fond memories.

Whatever you do, do not let Alone Grief engulf you. Fashion your own methods of keeping it at bay with something that will occupy you until it passes. We make choices in our lives and can either stay depressed or attempt to heal. Through our healing, we can then be supportive of others while keeping ourselves healthy physically and mentally. We can then get back into our routine with our families, friends and co-workers.

Grief impacts the family in many other ways. The divorce rate of a little more than 10% among bereaved parents, attributable to the death of a child, is much less than the 50% national divorce rate, but it remains a risk that needs to be addressed.

While you are taking care of yourself during bereavement, it is important to take care of your spouse and marriage. They will be grieving along with you and need your love and encouragement. Talk openly about your feelings with them so they know where you are at emotionally and how they can help you. No one can read your mind so they will need you to keep them informed. Encourage your spouse to talk to you about how they are feeling so you can support them, too. Do not be surprised if, at some point, one of you wants to talk and the other does not. You may be moving along in your grief at differing paces. What is important is that each of you is willing to listen when there is a need to express thoughts and feelings. Finding safe, effective means of coping with your grief such as talking things through with each other can be a healthy way to relieve your pain without additional marital strain.

CHAPTER TWO

One Day At A Time

GETTING THROUGH THE DAY, one day at a time, sometimes hour by hour, can be a challenge for grieving parents. Looking too far ahead or back into the past can be real pitfalls if the parent is not prepared for what can come of that. Taking your days incrementally, a proven method for many of the interviewees, is recommended. Plans must be made for learning to live life differently, without your child, for the family structure and history are forever changed when a child has died.

There will be many firsts after the child has died—the first monthly anniversary of the death, then on to the first year anniversary, the child's first birthday after the death, the first Easter, Thanksgiving, Christmas, the first family vacation, and so on. There are many other special days that families celebrated with their now-deceased child, depending on their personal family practices and religious and cultural backgrounds.

Some of the parents avoid those days totally, going away so they don't have to spend them at home. For them it seems easier to interact with strangers than family. Others prepare almost as if the deceased child is still with them, doing activities such as baking a cake to celebrate the child's birthday and preparing the child's favorite meal. One parent said that she and her husband buy each other holiday cards from their deceased child as if the child were buying them for them. Still others occupy themselves with something engrossing so they don't have to think about their loss. Parents should engage in what helps them get through those days, modifying their activities as needed.

Family celebrations and events take on a whole different feeling when a child has passed from their midst. The deceased child's absence is a huge cavern. Everything about the events looks and feels odd, different, sometimes strained, sometimes not. We make the effort to go on, trying to make it go as smoothly as possible for the grieving parents, friends, and family members such as the children of the deceased. Anecdotal evidence from grieving parents was that, while it was awkward at first, eventually new paradigms or patterns and new family practices emerge and become traditions. But the deceased is always missed.

Parents sometimes are placed in the position of having to answer questions about their children to new friends and acquaintances. One of the questions that may be asked is, "How many children do you have?"

Some parents were comfortable including the deceased child in the number without an explanation that one of their children had passed away. Others included the deceased child in the number, explaining that one of their children had died. Still others stated the number of children as only those who were living, not wanting to go into details about their loss. Parents rightfully answer in a way that is comfortable for them, giving just the amount of information they want to give.

There will also be the times when someone who does not know about the death of the child will ask the parents how the child is doing. At first it may feel as if cold water has been splashed on them. One can tell the inquiring person that the child has passed and accept the apologetic response politely, for no one asks such a question unless they care about you and your family. I have found it helpful to let the person know immediately it was okay that they asked. That makes the situation less awkward for all concerned.

Weeks after the child has died, parents will be cocooned in expressions of sorrow from well-meaning friends, family, and acquaintances. Eventually the attention tapers off. From the interviews I performed, some reported experiencing a point in time where they did not want to hear about the death anymore. Because of that and depending on where the parents are on the continuum, we must be sensitive to the responses that the grieving parents give when we talk with them. Guard against pressing them about their child if they signal or say that they do not want to address it. That does not mean that the parents do not want to discuss the child ever again, just that some do not want to talk about the death just then. That may very well change in the future and they will once again discuss their deceased child.

That also does not mean that it is too late for someone to express their sorrow about the child's passing if they did not learn about it right away. However, if the death occurred months ago, and, since some parents had a juncture after which it was unbearable for them to hear about it, it may be best to keep your sympathy expression short.

Being prepared to meet all of these challenges head-on will assist the grieving parents and their family and friends to have some measure of distraction on a daily basis and the ability to live with it, though not forgetting their loss.

The following recommendations are designed to assist grieving parents when they face days that trigger profound grief such as memories, birthdays, anniversaries, holidays and well-meaning but unsuccessful expressions of sympathy, from which they would like some measure of relief:

Planning For "Trigger Days"

▪   Plan ahead for trigger days to do something fun and engrossing so the mind is occupied. Recruit friends and family to be with you when possible.

▪   Make different or new memories on those days in order to overwrite what may have become unhappy ones. For instance, if your family has a specific holiday tradition, attend it, but do something different surrounding the event so as to create a new memory about it.

*   On these occasions, buy yourself something special or a treat. Make it a purchase that you would not ordinarily do for yourself but which is within your means.

*   When unhappy thoughts surface, train yourself to refocus onto something that is pleasant. Those unhappy thoughts could include bad things others might have said or done to you or your child, your own sense of failings, harsh words or hostility that may have occurred between you and your child or anything else related to the deceased that makes you upset. Remember the very best of times you shared with your child and block out those that make you sad. When the sad memories intrude, immediately switch them to the happy ones that you shared.

*   When you feel weepy, allow yourself a short period of time to cry, maybe fifteen minutes, then, if possible, make yourself stop it. The more you grieve deeply, the more depressed you can become. Get someone to support you in this endeavor and to help keep your crying within a short time frame.

*   If you are lonely, have no pet, and are able and want to get one, do so. Pets have been known to comfort their owners in ways that other techniques may not. They provide a warm body to listen to your sorrow, give unconditional love without judgment, and provide a place for owners to shower love and attention.

● If having a pet is unrealistic for you and you are lonely, go to a restaurant, the mall, or any other venue where people congregate. If being around people saddens you, then do something solitary.

● Learn what lifts your spirits and do that rather than doing what brings your mood down. Spend your time with people who can cheer you up and make you happy, rather than those who make you sad.

● Alert your family and friends if you think particular anniversaries are difficult. Enlist them to help you work your way through it. Make sure they understand what cheers you.

● When grieving or facing a trigger day, do not stay in bed all morning. Get up, get yourself cleaned up and practice good grooming. Doing so helps make a person feel better.

● Eat regular meals with others, if possible. Good nutrition is vital to good emotional health. Eating with others stimulates the appetite and breaks the "lonely cycle."

● Avoid alcohol on sad days. It is a depressant.

● If you find yourself alone a lot, patronize a restaurant, mall, coffee shop, or other establishment on a regular basis. The staff at these places generally interact in a friendly manner with regular customers.

● Do something for someone else, such as volunteering for something or doing charity work. This takes your focus off of yourself and your troubles and can cheer you up.

• Enjoy fellowship within your religious community regularly. They are usually supportive of their members, offering counseling and prayer.

• Get a hobby you enjoy and learn everything you can about it.

• Attend a support group such as the ones listed on the Resource Pages in this book. Members of these groups have shared experiences such as yours and will have ideas, which can help you.

• Do some kind of exercise when feeling down. Walking outside is particularly good as you are more likely to meet some people while getting exercise.

• Avoid sad movies, books, and television shows. They can trigger unhappy thoughts for you.

• Put away photos of your deceased child and objects that remind you of him/her if you find that they are making you feel sad. If keeping them out makes you happy, then do that.

• Whatever cues bad memories for you, make new, happy memories over it. For example, if going to a particular place reminds you of going there with your child, find someone else to go there with you or go by yourself until you have overwritten the sad memories with good ones.

If you try one of these methods or something else and are not immediately successful, take a break and retry the same methods. If success still eludes you with the method, try something else.

Do not give up.
Search out ways to try to feel better.

Remember, there are professionals who are trained in helping bereavement cases. Seek them out if the grief interferes with your activities of daily living, if you feel comfortable doing so.

The above suggestions are not all-inclusive but can assist grieving parents in making necessary changes in their lives. If you have other ways of keeping yourself from getting too down from your grieving, then use them.

Familiarize yourself with the many signs and symptoms of depression, some of which are insomnia, sleeping too much and feeling sad and tearful much of the day.

If you or a grieving parent exhibit any signs and symptoms of depression, get help immediately from a trained professional.

There will still be difficult times and sadness for grieving parents even if they practice proven methods, but the length of time of the sadness and also the frequency of the sad episodes can be reduced. What are offered are positive steps which can help us to decrease the amount of time we spend in harmful grieving. What is important is that we make a genuine effort.

Chapter THREE

What Works, What Does Not

APPROACHING A GRIEVING PARENT can be a daunting task for the rest of their community. Some people feel uneasy and, not knowing what to say or do, do not do anything. They may fear saying the wrong thing. That is disquieting to them and rightfully so. There are others who mean well but, lacking an understanding of the impact of their words and actions, say or do something that is uncomfortable for the grieving. Yet, some people strike just the right balance. The important thing is that you do something without being asked and that you follow the lead of the griever's response. Pay attention to the words and body language of the grieving parents. If they are sending signals that they need to be alone, graciously make your exit. If they do not appear to want to talk about their child's passing, then don't press them for information.

Part of the difficulty is that, unless we have suffered the death of a child, we can only imagine what the grieving are thinking and feeling. We do so from a point of view of what we "think" we would feel like should it happen to us. The truth is that no one can actually know what it is like to have a child die unless it happens to them. Those who have had a child pass away and offered to the grieving parents, "I know what you're going through because I lost a child myself," were well accepted.

Remember that weeks and months after the child's death, the parents will still be grieving, so continue reaching out to them with positive support. They will be facing the "firsts" such as the birthday of the child after their death. Taking them to lunch or calling them on these days would be appreciated. Listening to the grieving parent is one of the best things that someone can do for them. Recognize that their lives have changed forever. Obviously, comforting words and actions from friends and family are welcome regardless of what base the people are coming from. Throughout the interviews that I performed, people reported the many times others provided them with a measure of relief and peace through their actions, although there were people who did things that grieving parents found to be non-helpful.

One parent noted that it did not help when people judged how the grieving parent responded to their child's death. She said, "There was a real lack of understanding of how I was feeling and they talked badly about me because I didn't do what they thought I should do. That really hurt."

Grieving parents have the right to respond to their child's death in their own unique way, without criticism from others. It is their child who has died and their response is specific to them and their circumstances.
Respect that.

David's mother remembers that when people learned that her son passed away from AIDS, they wouldn't use the bathroom when they came to her home. That hurt her and her family.

More than one grieving parent was deeply hurt at how badly their family was treated because they were so upset they could not sit and talk with or entertain people who had come to express their sorrow at their child's passing.

There were interviewees who noticed that some people totally avoided them when they were in social gatherings. Real or imagined, the bereaved believed it was because people were uncomfortable around them. Make sure when you see grieving parents out in social settings, that you do not ignore them. Ask them how they are doing and whatever their answer is, let them know you are thinking of them and are glad to see them out and about.

The comforting outreaches that the interviewees received were many and varied.

Sandy was comforted by those who came to her home, brought food, said how sorry they were, and then left. "I didn't have to entertain them and that was good because I couldn't," Sandy said. Another who was interviewed did not want to see or hear from anyone.

Doris H. was comforted by a relative who called almost every week. That was healing for her.

Barb recalls the relief she experienced when friends took her shopping and to lunch, especially on her deceased child's birthday. It gave her an opportunity to focus on something other than her child's death.

Betty G recalls that she received a lot of comfort from the large numbers of people who came to her daughter's funeral. Other interviewees expressed the same sentiment. Betty G also appreciated that a local ambulance squad with whom her daughter worked flew a flag at half-staff for a month, and had a sign out front of their station in her child's memory.

Carolyn found that she was comforted when members of the medical community who cared for her daughter cried with her. She felt that it showed the compassion and understanding they possessed.

Lura was helped by others when they just came up to her and gave her a hug. She believes it showed that they had an understanding of her grief. For many, that was all they wanted.

Jim expressed the same sentiment. He appreciated the hugs.

Dianne and Mike appreciated when people cried with them.

One grieving parent was thankful when people gave her space and did not press her for comments about her child's death. "I just needed time to grieve alone," she said.

Throughout the interviews, I gained a sense of the deep appreciation that the parents had for those who had responded to their unique grieving situation. They believed that the way people helped them gave them a better perspective on how they could help other grieving parents in the future.

So, extend yourself to the grieving family with a prepared meal, a casserole, dessert, or some 2 liter bottles of soda or iced tea. Prepared food was always appreciated, especially if it was dropped off without an extended visit. If you are close to the family, offer to clean the house, pick up something that they might need, take them to lunch, or chauffeur them to places they need to go. If they have children, offer to baby-sit. If they need someone to look after their pets, make plans to do so. Just do something, make something, or send a card or a letter. Anything and everything is appreciated even if the family is too saddened to say so at first. And listen to them when they want to talk. When listening, don't impose your standards or expectations on them. Let the grieving grieve and ventilate their way.

The value of a warm, loving hug is underestimated. The interviewees all appreciated when they were on the receiving end of a comforting hug. They believed it showed compassion and caring and went a lot further than any words that were spoken.

Knowing something about the persons you are comforting and knowing what works and what doesn't work with grieving parents will help you determine how best to approach them at their time of loss. What is important is that you *do* approach them.

Chapter FOUR

What People Said That Helped, What Did Not

F OR THOSE WHO KNOW GRIEVING parents and wonder what to say to them, the lists below come from the interviews done for this book. They are in no way meant to be all-inclusive of what to say and what not to say, but rather reflect the experiences and opinions of the interviewees.

When reading from the lists, remember that some responses in each category helped some parents and did not help some others. They will be identified that way. Also, there were variations on all of the statements, so look at the message and read the interviews in Chapter Six of this book to assist you in understanding the impact on others of what we say.

Things Said That <u>Did Not</u> Help

1. You should not have had just one child.

2. You should adopt another child.

3. What can I do? (The interviewees want people to just do something, not ask what.)

4. I understand. (On both lists. To understand, you must be a grieving parent.)

5. Your child is in a better place. (On both lists. Before you say something like this consider if it will be well accepted by the person to whom you are speaking.)

6. Your child is now healed and enjoying a pain-free existence. (On both lists.)

7. It's God's timing. (On both lists.)

8. You must not have done what you should have done. (Judging the grieving never works.)

9. Do you have other children? You do? That's good. (The remaining children cannot replace the one who has passed.)

10. Get over it. It's been a year, you should be over it. (Judgemental, blunt and cold.)

11. Life goes on.

12. You can have another baby.

13. It was probably a blessing because there were going to be problems with the child, so it was for the best.

14. How could you have coped with another child who had a problem?

15. Don't worry about getting another baby room ready for your next one until you know everything is ok.

16. It's better in heaven than here. (On both lists.)

17. Your child will be fine. (On both lists.)

When you imagine yourselves as the grieving parents, you can understand why the above statements may not be helpful to them.

Things People Said That Did Help

1. God knows everything best.

2. It's better in heaven than here. (On both lists.)

3. Remember, your child is not suffering and has no pain now. (On both lists.)

4. He will be fine. (On both lists.)

5. I want you to know how much your child loved you.

6. I want you to know your child knew how much you loved him.

7. I'm praying for you.

8. Your child is in a better place. (On both lists.)

9. You're going to see him again.

10. The Lord will see you through this.

11. He was a special child and we were blessed to have him in our family.

12. It's God's timing. (On both lists.)

13. I understand some of what you are going through because I lost a child, too.

14. You were a wonderful parent to your child.

15. Your child is now healed and enjoying a pain-free existence. (On both lists.)

16. You are not alone. We are here for you.

17. Call me anytime. I will listen.

18. Let me tell you something good that I knew about your child.

19. I love your child very much and I know you do, too.

20. You must have been special because you had such a special boy on loan to you from God for a short time.

According to those interviewed, these statements provided comfort and solace for them. Again, these lists are not meant to be all-inclusive. They are intended as a guideline for another way to look at how our comments impact others.

You can read more about these statements in Chapter Six.

Chapter FIVE

Where Do We Go From Here?
How Do We Endure?
What Have We Learned?

P HILOSOPHIZING, ANALYZING, and reframing occupied my inner thoughts throughout my first few weeks after the memorial service for my son. No matter what I was doing, my inner voice, complete with video, was reworking what had happened from the first time I got the terrible phone call from Brandon saying, "Mom, I have a tumor." I especially replayed his last few days and what followed.

Other parents told me that they, too, replayed in their mind the last time they saw their child, the last things they said to each other and the last days or moments of their child's life and the days afterward.

As time passed, parents who lost a child began to wonder what other people did who went through the same loss. The questions are there without the answers. Is it worse if the loss was sudden or worse if your child lingered with an illness? 'What does it matter?' I would answer, the child is still gone.

After my ordeal, I began to think about all those parents who had said to me, "I understand what you are going through because I lost a child, too." That was helpful to me because I began to see true friendship and love in action through their sharing of their stories. As bad as it had been for them, I saw that they managed to get through each day, and now they were comforting me. It fostered hope.

Testimonies from others help us to understand how terrible the ordeal is for a parent regardless of what the circumstances are. In this book, we read their unique stories of how their son or daughter had passed away. Among the many interviewees, their deceased offspring passed at all ages—as babies, toddlers, children, and adults. No matter the age, the grief expressed was of a depth and breadth that had no boundaries. And often that grief was compounded by other stressors and struggles with which the family was dealing.

For these parents, there was no script for how to grieve or act after their child died and no instruction book for how to respond to this kind of loss and sadness.

And there is no policy and procedure for the correct way to work through such a tragedy. Through reading the stories in this publication, perhaps parents who face the death of a child will be able to gain some understanding of their own responses to their loss, find something to help them get through today, and give them hope to get up again tomorrow and endure.

Children of the deceased need to know that they will not be forgotten by their deceased parent's family. Keep in touch regularly with phone calls, E-Mails and letters. Celebrate their birthdays and holidays as you did before their parent passed. Pray for them and tell them you are doing so.

> ### The Grieving Parent
> ### Can Be Comforted In Knowing:

* You are not alone. Others stand with you in an attempt to help.

* God is ever present and will strengthen you.

* There are some common encounters and counsel that can ease your burden just a little bit, keeping you from further harm. Some of this is found in the stories herein and in groups such as those on the "Resource Page" of this book. Sometimes it is found with friends, family, churches and professional help.

* You are free to grieve your way as long as you don't harm yourself or others.

* While you will never forget your loss, time helps to ease the pain.

* Practicing your religion can bring you peace.

The days that we spent with our children included phone calls, visits, and working side by side with them. The days may now echo with hollowness. If so, the parents' responses to that void are varied.

How desperate could a parent get at the thought of working their way through life with no possibility of ever seeing their deceased child again in this life or ever hearing their voice again? Although all parents did not testify to experiencing thoughts of suicide, some acknowledged entertaining such an outlet and some admitted suicide attempts. Those whom I interviewed have since recovered from those feelings.

So where do we, as grieving parents, go on a daily basis for help from our grief? We can read the scriptures, pray, and talk out our problems with friends, family members and pastors, all of which can help. A personal religion was a life preserver for many of those interviewed. Our belief in God holds us up from the stormy seas, keeping us afloat with the hope that we will be supported in the pain and sadness we feel as we are being tossed about.

Other grieving parents were still grasping for something. Some of the interviewees attended groups for grieving parents and received support there.

❧   There are thousands and thousands of parents out there who have been through the same tragedy with all of the accompanying thoughts and feelings. We can let them help us when they offer and we can help others.

❧   We can be walking a particular path in life and all of a sudden a turn in the road appears and we must take it because that is the road we are on. So, we take it and find our way, day by day, struggling but persevering.

❧   Many parents who have lost a child carry guilt within their hearts for what they think they should have done or for what they did that they now regret. Once those feelings are faced and truth is separated from fiction, we can move on and try not to make the same mistakes again.

❧   Forgiving others and ourselves for real and perceived injury that we have caused or that was perpetrated upon us can be a healing experience. Guilt can be very damaging and feeds depression. It can consume our days and nights with senseless inner dialogue. When those thoughts arise, we must learn to refocus our thinking on something uplifting. The Apostle Paul tells us in Philippians 4:8 that we should be thinking about the good things in our lives. If a Biblical principal does not work for you, then you can attempt to refocus from your loss to something else that brings you joy. Most psychological therapies can be viewed as facilitating a learning to refocus.

❧   Dwelling on our loss without relief can lead to depression, and depression can lead to self-harm. People who suffer from major depression are more likely to attempt suicide.

❧   Believers can thank God for those blessings that remain in their lives, whatever they are. You can fill in the blank here for the many ways that God has given you to assist you to live and survive whatever comes your way. At the top of the list are family members.

＊   When you are able, open yourself up to the ones who would comfort you. Sharing the load with others makes our own burden lighter.

＊   Those whom our child left behind need us, too, no matter what their ages are. After all, many of us have surviving children, grandchildren, and other family and friends who need our love and support, too.

＊   Recognize that no matter what our age, we are learning something new. Strive to find ways to improve your lives and the lives of others. We are never too old to make a positive difference.

> *Within the stories in Chapter 6, the parents tell us what they have learned from their experience of losing a child.*

John and Rubena learned that, "If you have a relative or a good friend, tell them how much you love them," for you may never get the chance again. Dianne and Mike agree.

Betty learned the importance of having a will so that the possessions of the deceased are given to the ones they want to have them.

One parent learned that we must tell others how much they are appreciated before it's too late.

Joyce learned to be more compassionate and sensitive to other people. Especially those who grieve for children.

Babs learned that "The Lord giveth and he taketh and we must take it one day at a time and live for today."

Lisa learned that every parent's grief is different.

Judy learned that God is good and we should trust him.

One mother learned that practicing God's presence is comforting. She also learned that God is with us even when we don't feel his presence.

Each of the grieving parents interviewed learned something and mentioned it in their stories. Many say they are still learning. Our lives are forever changed and each day brings something new and is now formed by the loss of the child who is no longer with us.

This does not mean that we are without hope. Rather, the things we learn can point us to a different, more meaningful way of viewing the world. And as time goes on, the healing process brings more learning and some relief from the crescendo of conflicting emotions.

The experiences we encountered through all of this could embitter one were it not for that pure love from our Lord. We should not let such bitterness take root and grow. Instead, we must live in God's love and pass it on to others who are suffering, too. We never know when and where the grief-stricken will come our way.

CHAPTER SIX

Those Who Have Gone Before

WHAT A PRIVILEGE IT WAS FOR ME to interview the grieving parents and hear their bare-bones stories of raw grief, suffering, and hope. Each one had memorable stories about their child, some of which brought shared laughter. During the course of our visits together, their words were chosen carefully so as to present their truth and what they believe the readers should know.

Each story is painfully beautiful in the immeasurable volume of free-flowing parental love, directly from the heart. But the stories are in no way complete. Rather, they are just a snapshot of the universe of the complicated parent/child relationships we inhabit.

I am honored and privileged to have encountered, through their stories, the beautiful children of all ages whose tales are told in this chapter. While I never met them in this life, I feel as if I know a little bit about them through their parents' anecdotes. Their lives were bright flashes in our world and deserve to be heard by those of us who did not have the fortune to have passed their way. Each child is important, as are the coping mechanisms the parents used and the grief processes the parents have endured. These testimonies provide us with the opportunity to step away from our limited, confining view of what we believe should be, to what really is.

Read through the stories and hopefully, learning will occur both for and about ourselves. The parents' unique journeys are told in narrative form with their own words in quotes. Because of their honesty, an understanding is gained of the varied ways that parents grieve and how parental grieving is distinct from other grief that is experienced.

As you read non-judgmentally what the grief-stricken parents report, you will see the actions and words of well-meaning friends and family that work and those that may be ineffective or even offensive. You will also learn that other stressors within each family can compound the grief, and challenge their ability to cope. There is much more substance within each narrative that will speak to the reader, so follow them closely and open yourself up to hear what the families have experienced and what they desire the reader to know.

All of the precious children were deeply loved by their families and friends and through their parents' recounting of their stories, they will be of help to others.

Those Who Have Gone Before

Marsha Simone Linton
Age - 21
2/3/1972 - 8/15/1993

As told by: Ethlyn "Babs" Archibald,
Marsha's mother.

Marsha was born on February 3, 1972 in Jamaica, the only child of Ethlyn (Babs) Archibald. According to her mother, she was a fun-loving, kind-hearted child, characteristics that followed her through her life until she was killed in an automobile accident at the age of 21.

Right before the accident, Marsha had been in Russia on a scholarship from her place of work to study law. While there, she learned the difficult Russian language in six months and could read and write it. She was then planning on attending one year at Harvard, hoping to earn a law degree eventually. Becoming a lawyer was her childhood dream. When she was ten-years-old, Marsha taped herself acting as a judge and then as a lawyer, sounding as professional as she could.

Besides traveling, Marsha loved sports and did not want to be interrupted when watching them on television. Her mother knew better than try to ask her anything when one of her favorite teams was playing because her daughter was engrossed in the sports program.

Thumbing through the family scrapbook with Babs, I was struck by the six-foot-tall beauty whose zest for life jumped at us from the photographs. Her bright and smiling face peered out with a bold joy. There were pictures of Marsha with family, dancing with friends, at church functions, enjoying her life. Her poses and expressions attest to the love and fun of this sophisticated young woman.

Marsha returned to Jamaica after being in Russia. She enjoyed the outdoors and decided to go hiking with her friends on her last day of life, August 15, 1993. The eleven young women trekked up Blue Mountain and then back down again. While walking along the road, they were offered a van ride and they all piled inside for a trip together back to town. During the ride, the van was experiencing some engine troubles. At some point, the vehicle went over a precipice and Marsha was thrown out. Her friends heard her screaming and saw her body tumble over and over down the steep cliff until it came to rest below. Due to the rugged terrain, a helicopter was dispatched to bring her out and she was taken to University Hospital where she died at 8 p.m. that day. She was the only casualty of that accident.

At the same time of Marsha's accident, Bas was at work in a hospital in New York City. Throughout the night, she found herself singing a Jamaican burial song and was questioned about it by some of the staff. Babs had no answer for why that song was going through her mind but later wondered about the coincidence.

During her shift, a staff person told Babs that she should place a phone call to Jamaica. "What happened to Marsha?" was her reply. She knew immediately in her heart that something had gone terribly wrong for her child. She called a friend where Marsha lived and received the terrible news.

"I screamed and screamed and went into the nursing office," Babs says. ' "Marsha's dead," ' I screamed. One of the nursing staff took me home. Whenever I think about it, it's as if I'm right back there at that very moment."

"I had to go to Jamaican UWI hospital to identify her body. When I went in to see her, they pushed her body out and took a covering off of her face. I screamed and screamed, 'Oh God.' "

"I'm a God-fearing person," Babs says. "I deal with my problems by talking. I went back to New York City, was alone, and lost 100 pounds from grieving. It's one of those things where you believe it but you still can't understand that she is gone. After her burial I wanted to come back from Jamaica to the United States and went right back to work. I couldn't stay in the same apartment because it was several stories up and, feeling suicidal, I felt like dropping through the window. So I took a first floor apartment to help me to overcome that. I became depressed and didn't want to bathe or do anything. I don't feel like that now."

"Dealing with the patients at my work, doing the patient care, helped me feel better. I would look at the patients and relate to them, picturing myself as them, thinking, that could be me, sick in the bed. Being around people was helpful as was going to church.

Today, I picture my daughter as she looked when she

was alive and think of her as if she's still in Russia. That helps me to cope with her passing. And I can always talk about it. Sitting down with someone and talking about it helps.

Sometime later after her funeral, I went on a cruise and thought that would help me forget. I still thought of Marsha as being in Russia instead of being dead. I wanted to keep moving and doing things even though I felt like giving up but I knew my daughter would not like me to do that."

"One time, after going back to work on the 11p.m. to 7a.m. shift, I fainted at the nursing station. I ended up in the Intensive Care Unit suffering from stress because I was not resting and not eating. I cut down on the amount of days I worked part-time at the nursing home but continued my full-time hospital job. I wanted to be with people. I tried to forget what had happened."

There were things that Babs was doing that made her feel worse. "I became lonely," Babs said. "I do not have close contact with family where I am living here in Florida. I feel withdrawn, like I'm in exile."

People said and did things at the time of Marsha's passing, that they probably felt were helpful but Babs found did not help. Things like, 'You shouldn't have had just one child,' or, 'You should adopt another child.' "I told them that adopting another child cannot replace Marsha."

The things people said that were helpful were, 'God knows everything best,' and 'If God wants her alive, she would be alive.' "Some people said, 'It's better in heaven on the other side than here.' That helped me."

Faith played a large role in Babs' grieving process. "I am a God-fearing person. I like praying and I prayed. At first I couldn't pray but I learned to listen to God talk to me. I try to exercise my faith. I can always talk to God."

Coping with her daughter's passing is difficult. "Every day I think about it as if it was yesterday. I actually feel it in my body. I cannot take being around crowds because somebody there always looks like Marsha."

Has time helped? "A little. I'm not the same person now. As I get older, I'm not the same. It's different. Different. I thought that I'd be happier here but I'm not. I left New York and came here to Florida because I thought I'd be happier but I'm not."

"Grieving for my child is different from grieving for other family members or friends. You remember from the very first day that your child is born. It's different. You get a belly pain with the loss of your child."

"My only regret about how I grieved is that I did not stay in New York. I thought it would be better here and it isn't. It was okay for a while but then it got bleak. I have a lot of stressors. I want to go back to Jamaica."

"One thing I've learned from all of this is that the Lord giveth and He taketh. We must take it one day at a time and live for today. Thinking about nice things and making future plans helps me. I believe we should all give thanks for what the Lord has done. Who knows what the future could have held for Marsha? I just have to deal with it."

Babs and I looked at Marsha's books that she had shipped back to the USA from Russia. They ranged from Tolstoy to Russian language textbooks, a testimony to a well-read young woman.

Babs still thinks of her daughter as being in Russia.

Randi Lee Allison
Age - 24
1/25/1983 - 7/15/2007

As told by: Sandy and Bill Grubb,
mother and stepfather.

Randi Lee Allison was the younger of two daughters born to Sandy Grubb of Mims, Florida. Randi, 24-years-old, lived alone in a "smart house" designed for her, due to her being wheelchair-bound for 8 years following surgery after a car accident. She wore a torso brace and had a daily caregiver. Also living in her home was a renter of one of the bedrooms, a 20-year-old Ukranian man, Vitaliy Groesbeck.

Randi's dreams of her future life were cut short at the time of her car accident when she was 17 years old and in high school. She lived with her mother and stepfather Bill Grubb, for 5 years following her T-4 paralysis and they worried daily about finding her dead in her bed from her condition. Randi then moved into her own home where she lived for two years, so she could be more independent. On July 15, 2007, Randi, while sleeping, was shot in the head with a 22-caliber rifle sometime between 12 midnight and 2 a.m., allegedly by the renter. The case has not yet gone to trial.

After Randi passed, Sandy suffered a heart attack and also had cancer which added more stress to the situation.

Bill Grubb, Sandy's husband was the first of the couple to learn of Randi's murder. He had gone to breakfast that morning and passed Randi's home. He became concerned when he saw that the area around Randi's home was taped off and police cars were everywhere. "I knew without them telling me, what had happened," Bill says. It was Bill's responsibility to go back home and tell Sandy that her daughter was dead. "It is the hardest thing I have ever had to do in my life," Bill says. "I tried to be supportive and wanted to make this better but I couldn't. Now, I try to keep her occupied to help."

"Bill did all of that," Sandy says. "He sheltered me from everything. The police, the news people. He guarded me. We didn't read the papers or watch the news."

Sandy's initial response was to go into shock, a "take care of business mode," according to her. "Then it hit me when I went to the funeral home and I went into denial for a moment," she says. "It got worse after the first few months. I still feel I should pick up the phone and tell Randi something, or go see her. I realized at one point that, as a parent, my goal should be wanting the best for my child and so what was best for my child was to be in heaven and to be able to walk and do those things that she couldn't do here. So, if I wanted her with me that would be kinda selfish on my part. So, I constantly remind myself of that. Then the grief returns."

"With this week being the first-year anniversary of her death, life has been additionally tough. And of course, we have Randi's cat Rig-A-Maroo here. For the first three or four months, Rigs would get up on my bed and climb up and touch Randi's picture. She still does it once in awhile. She gets up on the end table and keeps her paw on a picture of Randi and falls asleep. She was in the house when Randi was shot so I don't know how that affected her. There are nights when I just have to cuddle the cat and I talk to Rig-A-Maroo about Randi. If I think about Randi, I talk to her. I don't try to pretend she's not gone because I know that she is but if I try to pretend that she's not gone, then I think I have to face the fact all over again that she is gone."

"When I think of Randi I picture her in the bed when she was paralyzed and I'm so proud of her because she was trying so hard and she was such a good, kind-hearted person. I am very proud of her."

Bill remembers how Randi went through a lot because of the car wreck and everything else she went through. "I'm a tough person," Bill says, "and Randi was, too. And strong-willed. I try to protect Sandy and the hardest thing was I couldn't fix this. I try to be supportive. At first she shut me out. She was mean, trying to cope with everything. So, I keep trying to do this better. We talk about it."

"It wasn't that I didn't want him around," Sandy says. "I just felt so much pain as the mother who bore this child who was ripped away from me."

Sandy appreciates how Bill understands that she sometimes needs alone time. "I am the only mother of Randi. No one knows what that means. No one can know how that felt to live as the mother of Randi. And it was very hard for me to open up that spot and allow other people in. Slowly, I came out of that. Bill would ask if there is anything he can do for me. I thought, you take care of you and leave me alone. I carried Randi, I nurtured her. I took care of her. Nobody in this world knows how I feel."

According to Bill, one of the best things that Sandy did to help her feel better was buying presents for other children with the money they would have spent on Randi's Christmas presents. Giving and helping others has helped them. On Christmas day, the couple went to a restaurant for breakfast. Sandy gave the waitress a $100 tip and also a $20 tip for each of the staff there, including the dishwashers. The whole month of December, Sandy and Bill gave to others. Sometimes, when going through the drive-through of a fast-food restaurant, they would leave the worker a $20 tip. "By helping others," Bill says, "We are helping ourselves, too."

"Another thing that made me feel better," Sandy says, "Was when I was at the funeral home, I went into the rest room and yelled at God. 'Why did you have to take her? I don't want her gone. I want her here with me. I want her back.' A parent shouldn't have to bury a child. Then I realized that was okay. God was strong enough to handle that. So, I can talk very honestly and openly to the Lord. I cry when I feel like it and allow myself to have whatever emotion I'm going to have. That makes me feel better. Sometimes I'll ask God to let me see her just once for a few seconds. I'll ask him to let me know she's okay." She's still waiting for that to happen.

There were things that made Bill and Sandy feel worse, too. "Telling myself what I coulda, woulda, or shoulda done was not helpful," Sandy says. "Even thinking like that is not productive. You're going to do that but you must counter it with something else."

People tried to reach out to the Grubbs after Randi's passing, and some things helped and some things did not. "I don't like it when they ask, 'What can I do?'"

Sandy says, "I can't be thinking about what they should do. Instead, they should just do something. Then, there were people who just stopped by, brought some food, said how sorry they were, and then left. I didn't have to entertain anyone which was good, because I couldn't. Everyone understood. I really liked it when people were saying, 'We're praying for you.' That was a wonderful thing."

Faith played a big part in Bill and Sandy's grieving process. "I talk to God about it when I want to," Sandy says. "He talks to me through the Bible and also to my heart. It's good to know that he's there. Randi's life would have been miserable with her limitations. She was a limitless person—a cheerleader, a basketball player. She made the best of everything. She lived life and now she gets to live again, just in a different place. And I'll get to see her again one day. People who don't have that, I don't know how they deal with it."

Grief counseling was offered because Randi was a murder victim but Bill did not attend. Sandy went to one session but did not go back because she felt that the counselor did not tell her anything she didn't already know.

Neither Bill nor Sandy has any regrets about how they grieved. "Even if it was wrong," Bill says. "I don't regret it. We all learn from what we do."

Coping with Randi's passing now continues to be a daily struggle. Talking to Randi has been helpful for Sandy. "Randi loved Snoopy so whenever I see a Snoopy toy," Sandy says, "I'll think of her and think it's like her saying she's ok. I don't care what other people think about that. If they don't understand, I don't care. Opinions are just that and everyone has a different one."

Bill made a beautiful memorial garden in memory of Randi for Sandy to go sit in. He put a waterfall feature in it, which he believes Randi helped pick out. Also included in it are a Snoopy statue, a bench, and Randi's favorite flowers. There's a statue of a little girl that Bill bought that Sandy says looks a lot like Randi did when she was little. Sandy enjoys going there to sit and talk with her deceased daughter. She finds it helps her cope. Soon, Randi's ashes will be placed in the area.

Bill copes by taking care of Sandy. "As a guy," Bill says, "I want to say, 'Just get over it.' Don't say that, guys. Just be there. The only thing I do is I tell her when she appears to be getting too depressed or feeling sorry for herself too long. I mention it to her and say, 'That's enough now.' You have to be able to talk about it or you'll be divorced. And I tell Sandy not to forget her other daughter."

For the one-year anniversary of Randi's passing, Bill made arrangements for them to attend a display that Sandy wanted to see in Orlando. He planned it to take her mind off the memories of what happened.

Grieving for Randi was different for Sandy and Bill than when they lost other friends or family. Both found Randi's death more shocking than any others that they experienced. "When somebody gets murdered," Bill says, "You have no warning, you don't expect it."

"When mother passed," Sandy says, "I had three sisters to help me grieve. When Randi died, I was the only mother of Randi, and I hurt. A part of me was alone in the world with that knowledge. No one knows what that means. No one knows how that felt to be the only mother of Randi. Nobody knows how I feel. I never saw Randi dead even though there are pictures. I just wanted to remember her as she was when she was alive."

To the readers, Bill wanted to repeat the message that they should not say, 'I shoulda, coulda, woulda, done something.' "Thinking of things you could have done doesn't help."

Sandy wants the readers to know that they should not put off things that they want to do. And she wants people to understand that only the mother knows how she feels and to be patient with her. "You don't owe anybody anything at that point. You only owe it to yourself. If I helped anybody in anything, it would be to understand that it's ok to have these feelings you experience. The intensity won't last. It will be there because you lost a part of you and you can't ever get it back. Don't back away from it. Face it. I know God won't give you more than you can handle so apparently I'm pretty tough. I learned how strong I am."

"Everything happens for a reason," Bill says. "I believe that. And I'm sure this would cause a great many divorces, especially if people aren't secure in their relationship."

"And I have a philosophy that you can't enjoy the mountains," Sandy says, "If you haven't been through the valleys."

Postscript:

Randi's murderer, Vitaliy "Alex" Groesbeck was found guilty of Second Degree Murder on October 29, 2009. He is due to be sentenced on December 11, 2009.

Jeannette "Tracy" Talbot Smith
Age - 19
9/25/1959 - 7/2/1979

As told by: Anita Kirk, Tracy's mother

Tracy Talbot Smith was a fun-loving young woman who had a talent for languages. She lived in Bournemouth, England where the gifted student finished high school at the age of 16. Brussels, Belgium was where Tracy spent her last year of life, attending language school. At the age of 19, she passed all of her language courses with Honorable Mention but was unaware of it because she died before the grades were announced.

Tracy lived in an upper apartment of a doctor's city home while at the Brussels language school. In exchange for her lodging, she tutored the doctor's sons in English. The day before Tracy's passing, the doctor and his family were having tea on the lawn of their country home. At one point, the doctor noticed that Tracy wasn't paying attention. He asked her about it and she said that for a moment she could see him and hear him but she had no idea what he said. Tracy said that it was like a flash. Nothing more was mentioned about it and they packed up and went back to their city home. Since they arrived late, Tracy went up to her apartment. That's the last anyone talked to her. The next morning, she didn't come down for breakfast and the family was concerned. The doctor rang the long, old-fashioned bell on the stairs that was used to summon her to come down. When she didn't arrive, the doctor went up to find out why. He went inside the apartment and discovered that Tracy was dead. The police, ambulance and doctors were called because Tracy died in another country other than her home country of England. An autopsy confirmed she passed about 5 a.m. from a burst aneurysm. Tracy's father did everything that had to be done after she died because her mother Anita was traveling and they were unable to contact her.

Tracy was cremated in Belgium and her ashes were brought back to England before Anita even knew she had passed. A memorial service was scheduled for a later date to provide time for someone to contact her mother.

"Larry (Anita's husband) and I were traveling around southeastern United States in a motor home when Tracy passed away," Anita says. "We were driving through North Carolina, Georgia, Florida and Louisiana as we made our way to New Mexico for Larry's next assignment. We weren't in touch with anybody until we got to New Mexico so we didn't immediately know that she had died."

When the Kirks finally got to New Mexico, Larry processed in, and the Red Cross alerted him to what had happened. He came back to where he and Anita were staying and told her about Tracy.

"I couldn't believe it," Anita says. "I just didn't believe it. I said, 'There's no way that could happen.' I didn't believe it. I screamed and screamed and screamed and said, 'No, No, No, it can't be true.' I called family members and found out that it was true. It was a terrible mess. Horrible."

Anita felt as if she had let her daughter down by not being there for her.

"I didn't believe it could be true because Tracy and I recently had a wonderful, wonderful visit together in Brussels," Anita says.

Like many others, Tracy's story is not without a mystical anecdote.

"At the Brussels airport when she and I parted," Anita says, "I was going down the escalator and we were laughing. Tracy all of a sudden got quiet and tearful and said to me, 'Mommy, I'm never going to see you again.' I said, 'You silly twit. Don't be so silly, why are you saying that?' It was as if she knew something that I didn't know. It was impossible for me to believe what she just said because she had already made plans to come see me in a couple of weeks."

Everything was planned for Tracy to come to the USA to work as an interpreter for a company. She was going to have a quick visit with her mother before she started her first real job.

"She wanted to travel," Anita says. "She wanted to fly and one of her dreams was to see San Francisco. Tracy and I spoke on the phone after I arrived home because she wanted to make sure I got here all right. I received a letter from her every single day." Some of those daily letters that Tracy wrote arrived after her death because of the delay of mail between Brussels and the USA.

Now, Anita asks questions of God. "Why would he take somebody like Tracy and leave a wretch like me?" she says. "Why is that? When you see evil and cruel people living and good people are gone. Why is that?"

She also thinks about the real meaning of this world. "Some people say that this is your hell," she says. "That your hell is on earth. I don't know what I believe anymore."

Tracy's death has caused her to doubt the God she was raised to believe in. "I was brought up in a very religious family. We went to church on Wednesdays and three times on Sunday. After Tracy died, I lost it. I can't believe that I'm still here and she's not. I still have doubts."

Despite all that, Anita believes that the life Tracy led was a good one. "Tracy had all the joys of life and none of the ills," Anita says. "Her biggest disappointment in life was when her father and I got divorced. I have guilt feelings about that, too. Maybe if I hadn't divorced, I'd have been there for her."

She continues to question why God didn't take her instead of her daughter. "I'd been so close to death so many times and God didn't take me. Why not? Why take her? Tracy had her whole life ahead of her. She could have done so much good in the world. She would have been a shining star. She would have done great things in little ways. She would have been a wonderful, caring, helpful, devoted individual and she didn't get that chance. And I didn't get no grandbabies. But I am looking forward to the day I see Tracy again."

Tracy's passing affected Anita in other ways. "For a long time, I hadn't been able to go to a funeral after Tracy died. But the time came that, for particular reasons, I had to go to one so I did. I tried on other occasions but just couldn't attend. Not even if it was a close friend or family member. My family understood and thought it was okay but other people thought it was terrible and they said, 'If I died, you won't come to my funeral?' I said 'probably not.' I can't cope with death."

Before long, depression set in. "As the months went by I was depressed, tearful, sad," Anita says. "Just totally hurting. I wasn't happy that I had no part of her memorial service or anything. And when the time came for attending it, I couldn't get on the plane and go. I couldn't go. So, that was bad, too. Then I felt guilt over that and some family blamed Larry but it wasn't his fault. Some still believe it was. I was in an emotional hole for a long, long time. And I couldn't go to a funeral for years after that. You see other people just get on and go and get over it."

In time, Anita found ways that helped ease her pain. She handcrafts beautiful one-of-a-kind dolls. "Being creative in some way helps me," She says. "That was one way that took me out of this. Even though reading Tracy's letters made me feel sad, it also made me feel better. I put all of her letters and photos in a box and every now and then I take the letters out and spread them around and read one of them. It helps me. Now I can do it much easier. Before, the sadness would take over for days and days. I had never been diagnosed for depression but I am sure I had it. My husband was very supportive and understanding but my grief went on too long. As her pictures were sitting around in different places in the house, I was dwelling in that grief. Putting them away helped me to start living again. Grieving for Tracy was different than other grief I experienced because of the closeness she and I had."

Anita experienced times of outreach from others, all of which was not helpful. "People said things such as, 'I understand,' which did not help, because they don't," she says. "They don't have a clue. I've said that myself in the past and now I find myself trying not to say it." Another thing that was hurtful was the lack of understanding from friends when she didn't get on the plane and go to Tracy's memorial service. "That did not help," Anita says. "There was only one friend who understood."

What helped? "I think that the only help that I felt

was from my husband Larry. I don't feel I got a lot of support from others."

She finds that the funerals she attended here in the USA are different from her home country of England. "Everybody goes to a big meal afterward and they have conversations unrelated to the deceased. It is like the deceased isn't even there. I couldn't do that."

Anita continues to ask "Why" questions. "Why did the wicked people live and Tracy is gone?" she wonders. "I can't believe in God anymore for doing that. Why do you take this wonderful person here and leave the wicked? I have a lot of those questions constantly. That's why I don't believe there is a God anymore." She believes that if there were a God he would have been there for her daughter and wouldn't have let it happen. "If he had to have a body or a soul," Anita says, "he could have taken another soul." She is no longer convinced that there is a heaven and a hell, either. "I don't know," she says.

Anita didn't attend any grief counseling although a local church and the Red Cross offered. She didn't want it because she didn't want to talk to anyone.

"Now, after all these years, I still have my sad times along with my happy times," Anita says. "I think about all the fun things and how beautiful Tracy was and how much fun she was. At times I have felt like she was actually here with me for a minute."

One big regret remains for the grieving mother. "I wish I had been more accessible to others. Looking back, I don't know that I would have been, but I wish I had not been so closed up and shut everyone out. I wish I would have gone and talked to a minister and a counselor. But my way of coping was to run away and hide like it didn't happen. Not believing it even though I knew it happened. I crawled into a hole and stayed there a long, long time."

Many things were learned from everything that happened. "I learned that I was a good mom," Anita says. "And Tracy thought I was a good mom which was very important. I learned a lot of things I would do differently. I learned how it is to be heartbroken, to feel bad, to hurt, to love. I've learned about forgiving. I've learned recently now that life is very short and you have to make the most of each and every moment and each and every person in your life and it's not that bad. That you can recover from this. Even though you stay sad. I try to hide it so Larry doesn't know I'm feeling sad. That's when I'll take out her letters and photos and talk to her and I'm fine for a while then. I'll read maybe just one letter. I'll just pull it out and I'll read it. It's like she's talking to me. Like she's right there. I think it helps now. I don't think you ever forget what happened. I won't say the pain lessens. You learn to deal with it. I have fun times and I laugh. I'm very sensitive to things, more sensitive than I was, and I easily cry now where I didn't before."

Does Anita have anything to say to others who are grieving the loss of a child? "I would say, 'enjoy the wonderful memories and treasure all those special times that you did have together. Because they do help.' Everybody has different relationships with whomever they have lost and there's always happy times or sad times. You might be sorry for times you got mad at them but those times are part of life."

Mackenzie Leigh Young
Age - 7
10/17/1996 to 11/03/2003

As told by: Lisa and Dwayne Young, Mackenzie's mother and father.

Lovely, seven-year-old Mackenzie Leigh Young suffered from a mitochondria disorder, a cell deficiency that does not enable people to put on fat or muscle tissue correctly. Because of this affliction, she was paralyzed and unable to care for herself. This fun-loving little girl had thick black curly hair and an olive complexion. Most of her days were spent in a wheelchair with others providing her care.

Lisa, Mackenzie's mother, found herself focused on Mackenzie when she was in the hospital in Orlando for treatment while her husband Dwayne was left with all of the family responsibilities in their Palm Bay home. Dwayne would get his other two daughters up and ready for school, take care of the home and the bills, and then go off to his job. Sometimes in the evening, the family would travel to the hospital to visit Lisa and Mackenzie. "I had to do everything here," Dwayne says, "Then I would travel over to the hospital to take Lisa some food or items she needed. I would get her situated, then come back home, and make sure the girls got up the next morning for school."

The strain of the distinct but separate parental responsibilities and workload placed a strain on their marriage. "It was tough, and it was hard. We were growing apart," Dwayne says. "We weren't focusing together as a team and our marriage was on the rocks. Then Mackenzie passed and everything came back to center. It brought us so close. Lisa was there for me. She was my support. And I was there telling her it's okay to cry in front of me. 'You don't have to hide your emotions in front of me. I'm your husband.' We were focused. Our marriage has been a lot stronger and a lot better since then. It drew us back together where we were one again."

"The image of the day she passed is clear in my mind until this day," Dwayne says. "I was the one who would check on Mackenzie in the morning because we didn't know how long she would live and Lisa didn't want to be the one to find her dead. I put her to bed the night before she passed. She said the word 'Mom' clearly that night which was unusual. I got chills from that and put her in bed with Lisa who picked her up and hugged her and started crying. When I asked her if she wanted to go back to her bed she said 'yeah,' which, again, was clear for her. I gave her a kiss and I prayed with her. I held onto her little hand and I asked God to please make her pain stop. The following morning when we woke up. Lisa said 'don't go in the room and check on her right away.' I said 'okay,' because when Mackenzie gets up, she gets all of our attention and we still had to get the other children ready for school. I stepped one leg into the shower and I heard Lisa scream, "no, no, Mackenzie's dead.' I ran across the hall into her room and I reached over and touched her and I saw that she was dead. I could feel that she had been gone. It was tough making the phone calls and telling all the family."

"And I kept asking Dwayne when they were coming to take Mackenzie out of the house because I didn't want everyone seeing her dead," Lisa said.

"I went from being hysterical and upset to being mad," Dwayne said. "I had gone out of the house after Mackenzie died to meet the paramedic and police who had come. Then I wanted to get right back inside to see her again but a policeman blocked my way. Now I understand how people need to see their loved one and have closure. I needed to see her and touch her and know she really had passed. Lisa was the opposite. She had accepted her death and didn't want to see her again."

"I remember everything that happened that day but I don't remember her," Lisa says. "I don't remember what she looked like or what happened at the funeral home."

"I remember everything clearly," Dwayne said. "Soon after, our younger daughter said she wanted to call God and talk to Mackenzie. I explained that it doesn't quite work that way. You just talk to her through your prayers, I told her. We told her that Mackenzie would be listening. Our daughter yelled out, 'Mackenzie, I love you,' and the water on the kitchen sink turned on all by itself and starting running. Our daughter said, 'I knew she would hear me.' Even though Mackenzie had passed, our daughter told us that Mackenzie would come and sit and talk to her and play with her. She told us that she would come back again. Now that she is older, she doesn't talk as much about it as she use to. Lisa got jealous of our younger daughter having these interactions with Mackenzie."

"I wanted so badly to experience those things," Lisa said. "As a grieving parent, you sometimes look for things."

"Once when I was in church with some relatives, I felt Mackenzie on my back, just like when I use to put her on my back and carry her around when she was living," Dwayne says. "The feeling lasted for about 20 minutes and I didn't want it to stop. Another time, I got the feeling that she was on my back when I was in my car. I pulled off the road to enjoy the feeling. After I got back on the road, I came across a bad car accident. I honestly believe that it was Mackenzie and that she was doing that so I wouldn't be in that wreck. A couple of times we saw a blur that looked like Mackenzie going across our living room and we'd look at each other and say, 'did you see that?' "

After the initial shock of Mackenzie's passing, the grieving experience was different for Lisa than it was for Dwayne. "As a mom, I knew I couldn't change what happened and I had to be thinking of my other children. When people would come here, bringing food or just to visit, I would ask, 'Why are they here?' I didn't want anyone here. I wanted to get back into our schedule. I just went on. The girls went back to their cheerleading. I never lay there and cried and cried. I got up and got dressed and went back to my routine. I fought my emotions and thought I couldn't deal with it."

"She would cry when we went to bed at night and no one was around," Dwayne says. "And she would tell me things that were very hurtful to me. It made her really mad that I put Mackenzie to bed and was the last person to see her alive. I know that was her way of grieving but that hurt me. I was a mess."

"I remember telling his mother that he has got to get it together," Lisa says. "He was driving me crazy. I just thought that he had to stop his grieving."

"Everything medical had to come out of Mackenzie's room the day she died," Dwayne says. "I was just mad that she had to go through all that. I carried it all out by myself, loaded it into a van and gave it away. I was an emotional wreck. Mackenzie was my best friend. Lisa had cheerleading with the other daughters to go to and I would spend that time with Mackenzie. We watched all the television shows together and I would talk to her, telling her how my day went. We'd hold hands or I'd take her out of her wheelchair and put her on my lap. I lost that. I was confused. Lisa still had the cheerleading competitions to go to with our other daughters and I had lost what I had. I didn't like the change. I was an emotional wreck. I went to the doctor and he put me on meds. I had lost my job shortly after Mackenzie died so I had that extra problem which made me more depressed. So, I went hunting with my dad, came back and got another job. That was good because it broke up my routine and made me focus on something else. I think I'm a very emotional individual and don't hold anything in where Lisa is more personal about her grief. I was grieving 24 hours a day. I grieved everywhere. I'd be up during the night and sleep during the day."

Lisa says, "I was going on with my life for our other daughters. I kept pushing him and pushing him to get over it. I wanted him to see it my way. I begged and pleaded with him to get over it. So, I put Mackenzie's services together quickly so that we could get on. I didn't do a viewing for the public because I didn't want everyone remembering her that way. In our family, people said, 'but everyone has to say goodbye.' And I said 'no, they don't.' See, in my family, the funeral services are a huge, drawn out thing for a week. People are at the house, there are pictures taken, even of the deceased. I didn't want that. People would say, 'you need to cry,' and I would want them to get away from me. I'm a firm believer that when God deals you a hand, you do the best you can with that."

"What actually brought me out of my meltdown was my getting a new job that I had to focus on," Dwayne says. "I still have battles even after all this time. Sometimes I cry when I look at her picture. It's hard. It's your child. Our child is not here to hold. We wanted to keep Mackenzie here for selfish reasons instead of letting her go."

There were things that they did which made them feel better. "When I had free time," Dwayne says, "I would go down to the cemetery and look at Mackenzie's plaque. It is quiet there. I enjoy that. Lisa doesn't like doing that. And we took in foster care children to try to help them."

"For me, what helped was the foster care, where we have taken in kids with special medical needs," Lisa says. "We only have each child for a little while but it is something I can do."

"And adopting the boys helped," Dwayne says in reference to the two little boys, brothers, that they have adopted into their family since Mackenzie passed.

"I learned from my aunt who lost a child, that people are going to tell you that they know how you feel," Dwayne says. "And we know that they don't know how you feel but they mean well by it. It's not like when a grandparent or other relative dies. This is different. People have said to me, 'I don't know how you go on or how you can stand it losing a child.' I tell them, I have two other daughters who need me. With others responding to her death, you are going through a huge range of emotions. It's so hard. Sometimes you are sad, and other times you're mad or in disbelief. You're not supposed to make plans to bury your daughter. You have to think of your other family members, too, how at one moment they might be happy thinking about the good times with your daughter and you are maybe in a different stage where you are feeling sad about the loss. Everyone in your family may be at a different place in their grieving. They might be grieving at a different pace or having a different emotion."

"Mackenzie had a sense of humor," Lisa says. "She would laugh about the dog or her sisters. She sometimes pulled her sisters' hair and then she would laugh."

"I tell people that I can relate to how they feel but I don't really know what they are feeling," Dwayne says.

"Even though, with losing a child, you have similar feelings. We had our child for seven years, who was medically challenged and fragile. It was terminal but they didn't give us a date or time when she would pass. After she made it past the age of four, we wondered how much longer she had because that's when we were told she would deteriorate and die. Other people have different experiences with losing their child because they may have only had them for one day or maybe their child didn't pass until they were an adult."

"We had trouble making decisions about the funeral," Lisa says. "Should we have a viewing? I said 'no.' I thought it was nobody's business what she looked like. But we finally agreed on having just the immediate family for a viewing. I can't remember now who was really there. I know there were hundreds of people there for the funeral but I can't remember much about it. There were a lot of medical people there who had worked with Mackenzie and I remember them but that's all. And after the funeral, that weekend, our other daughters had a cheerleading camp and people there kept saying to us, 'I'm sorry,' and I'm like, 'Why? She's not stuck here anymore.' At that moment that's where we were coming from. We were grasping for anything after she passed away. I remember when anybody gave us a book about the other side or heaven, Dwayne would just eat it up. I looked at him wondering because he was raised religiously and I wondered if he was questioning all that. Now I realize that was okay, too. He seemed to need to have it in black and white. After reading some of those books, I pictured Mackenzie just running and saying, 'here I am,' being the person she was inside that body."

What made them feel worse? Dwayne recalls his wife being mad at him after Mackenzie passed because he had been the one who had put their daughter to bed the night before she passed. "I know it was just the way she was grieving but little things like that, that she would say hurt me, on top of everything else and losing my daughter. I know it was just her way of dealing with it. She was going through the anger stage at that point and she was redirecting it at me instead of dealing with just being angry at the situation. Stuff like that was hard."

Dwayne dealt with the grieving process differently than his wife. "I was open and crying and it drove her crazy."

"I was raised differently," Lisa says. "Everyone thought I should have some down time. But, because of the other children, I didn't want any down time. I still don't do down time. When I was riding in the car I had to listen to stations that were only upbeat because I would relate every single thing with Mackenzie. Then you start playing tricks on yourself and I'd relate everything to her. I'm part Cherokee Indian and I have a sign for each of my daughters," Lisa says. "Mackenzie was my butterfly. The day she passed, butterflies were everywhere. Every single day I see a butterfly since she passed and it's been five years and I think of her because that's something that I relate to her."

Dwayne found the same thing happening to him. "The only day I didn't see a butterfly was when I went up north hunting and it was cold outside. But even on some of those days, there still was a butterfly and it was like, 'whoa, that reminds me of Mackenzie.' "

For Mackenzie's parents, there were definite things that people said and did that were not helpful. "When they would tell you that they knew how you feel," Dwayne says, "That was not helpful. They did not know how we feel."

"Dwayne would not say anything," Lisa says, "but I would say, 'oh really?' And Dwayne would grip my arm tight. I would get angry."

"I would get angry, too," Dwayne says, "because they don't know how we feel." "There was a time that we went out to eat and the waitress asked where our daughter in the wheelchair was, and it just hurt us. Then my younger daughter said, 'She died,' and the waitress was upset.

"We still run into people today who don't know Mackenzie died and it's a reminder," Lisa says. "I wonder why the whole world doesn't know. We had this beautiful van that was outfitted for Mackenzie's wheelchair but after she passed I told Dwayne I was not driving it anymore. I couldn't get in that driver's seat and look in the rearview mirror and not see her. I never got back into that vehicle again. I remember one day he asked me to back it out and I said 'no.' "

"I kept two of the seats we had in it and put them in my truck," Dwayne says. "The one chair Mackenzie originally sat in and for a lot of times when I drove to the store and someone wanted to sit in that chair, I said 'no. That's Mackenzie's seat.' It was weird but that's how I felt."

Faith played a large role in their lives. "My faith helped me a lot," Dwayne says. "I turned to the minister for help and I looked at it that she's not suffering and she's not in pain anymore and she's able to run and play and do all the things which she wanted to do. And that's something that I kept trying to focus on. It helped me when I started realizing that because I was mad and I was hurt."

"When I picture Mackenzie now," Dwayne says, "I picture her the same age as she was when she passed and I picture her playing and smiling down on us and not suffering and not in pain."

"My faith was pretty much the same," Lisa says. "Except that Dwayne is convinced that I don't want to go to church now because I'm mad. That's not why. It's because my older daughter didn't want to go."

"We went from going to church a lot, to now it's a battle to go to church," Dwayne says.

When asked if she was mad at God, Lisa says, "No. On Saturday nights Mackenzie liked to go to church because of the music. But my older daughter wouldn't go now so I wouldn't go. I think she was mad at God and is now still a little frustrated. She was a kid then but she's matured."

"The reason we're still in this house," Dwayne says, "is because of the other children. This is the house Mackenzie lived in and they don't want to move from it. So we're putting an addition on the house for the space we need rather than move."

Going to grief counseling was an option. "The girls went and they were evaluated and then they went to a grieving camp," Lisa says. "Neither of them have ever been away from our family for any time and that was tough. They didn't want to stay because they didn't want to do the grief exercises."

Dwayne and Lisa went to counseling both together and apart. "They wanted us to go to a candlelight service with other grieving parents and we didn't want to go. We had a special-needs kid who died of a medical issue. My kid was stuck in a body that she actually hated so I decided not to do it. Dwayne supported me on it. Mackenzie couldn't tell me if she had pain or what she wanted to eat or anything. I can't be selfish about it because she's free. We chose not to go back to counseling. Dwayne and I had to come to terms that we were dealing with it in totally different ways."

How do they cope now? "I stay busy being a mom," Lisa says. "And if anybody asks me questions about Mackenzie, I like talking about her. I temporarily take care of medically needy children for the welfare system, too."

Grieving for their daughter's passing was different for them than for the grieving that they have done for other family or friends. "Definitely, I do believe it's different," Lisa says. "This grief was a lot stronger. I tried to be strong for my other children. Everyone looks at Dwayne and they think he's this big strong guy but I was like a mother lion, protecting Dwayne and the girls. I would go to the shower and cry because that was a private place for me. Dwayne caught me once and asked if I was crying. I told him 'no.' Then I got to taking two showers a day so I could cry in there but Dwayne was catching on to it. It sounds quirky but it worked."

"The grieving for Mackenzie was a lot stronger than any other grief I ever experienced," Dwayne says. "There's no comparison losing a child to losing someone else."

Any regrets about how they grieved? "Now I wish I wouldn't have been so protective because my older daughter might have grieved differently," Lisa says. "My younger daughter did fine but my older daughter doesn't want to talk about it. She just says, 'I'm fine. Don't talk to me about it.' I feel like she didn't get to grieve for her sister. She could do anything medically for Mackenzie that I could do. She wasn't scared of it. If I would have been open about grieving, maybe she would have been. Even with the school counselors, she says, 'I'm fine.' She kept on the Honor Roll all the way through."

And did they learn anything from this experience? "I would say I learned every person's grief is different," Lisa says. "I had to learn that Dwayne was a mush about grieving and that it was okay. I would maybe not protect the children as much and I would let other people help me when they wanted to instead of saying no. I learned that I have to be in control and that when I can't control people's emotions that would unnerve me. And that I'm very schedule oriented."

Dwayne says they have specific ways of coping with their loss now. "We try not to think of the pain and suffering, instead we try to think of the good times, her smile, and the positive impact she had on everyone that she was in contact with. I think of how she reached out and touched so many lives. I think that she's no longer in pain and she's not suffering. She can do the things she always wanted to do. She's no longer a bright child trapped in a body like she was. She was a prisoner in her own body. She's not like that anymore."

Do the Youngs have any regrets about the way they grieved? "I guess I may have upset Lisa with my grieving process and I wish that wouldn't have happened. It was just our different ways of grieving," Dwayne says.

The couple believes they have learned many things from the whole experience of losing their daughter and the grief they encountered. "Enjoy your children while you have them," Dwayne says. "Because you never know, you might lose them tomorrow. Live each day and enjoy those moments. Even when they are driving you crazy."

Lisa says, "I felt like I got better every day. The year before Mackenzie passed away, I was with her 24/7 because she was often in the ICU. Dwayne didn't get to do that. I didn't give him the option to do that. He would come and offer to relieve me so I could go take a shower and I would say 'no.' I had all that time with her that now I wish I would not have cheated him out of. I also learned that everybody grieves differently. I had to learn that is okay."

What would this couple want others to know about grieving parents? "I think they have to be open to accept the way that you are going to grieve," Lisa says. "Don't fight it or try to do the opposite of what you really feel you should be doing or it won't work for you. Like for me, I try to be strong and that is still working for me after all these years. I just tell myself to 'get real.' It works for me."

Dwayne wants people to know that whatever you feel, is right for you. "Don't take everything everyone says and think you have to live that way. If you feel you need to cry, you cry. If you feel you need to yell, then you yell. That's what I told other people. As a policeman, I take the calls where people pass away because since my daughter passed away, I feel I can help."

Kelly Dawn Heuer
Age - 7 ½ Months
7/31/1968 to 2/17/1969

*As told by: Doris and Keith Heuer,
Kelly's mother and father.*

Sweet Kelly Dawn Heuer lived her short life as a happy, smiling baby despite having Werdnig-Hoffman disease. The disease deteriorated her spinal column leaving her unable to hold her head erect or move her left arm.

Kelly's father Keith had been seriously injured in a car accident prior to Kelly's birth. He endured double amputation of his legs and multiple hospitalizations so the couple was overjoyed when their daughter was born. They started with a new life and new family and looked forward to their future lives together.

One of the first indications that there was an issue with Kelly was when they took their child to get her photographed and the photographer asked them if she could hold her head up. The answer was no.

Upon returning from a visit to Gramma and Grampa's home, Doris could tell that her daughter was not feeling well. She put the child in her carrier and went to fix her a bottle. When she came back, Doris picked Kelly up and knew instinctively that something was wrong. Doris and Keith took their baby to a doctor who examined her thoroughly and provided treatment for the fever she had. Kelly was admitted to a children's hospital in Buffalo because the physician said she needed to be seen by specialists. Kelly's parents believed that she was going to recover because, "My mind wouldn't let me think anything but positive thoughts," Doris says.

The specialists informed Doris and Keith that their daughter was very sick and would not recover. Upon her last hospitalization, the doctors tried to prepare them for the fact that their daughter was not going to survive. Keith accepted the doctor's decision but Doris just could not accept it.

"I didn't want her to be alone when she passed," Doris says. "When the hospital staff sent me home, I went but I didn't like to do it. I really didn't want to go home."

"The last night before she passed," Keith says, "they sent us both home about 1 a.m.. I knew she didn't have more than a couple of days."

"At 2:15 a.m.," Doris says, "we got the call that Kelly had died. The nurse said there is no use coming in and I said 'yes, we are coming in.' "

Doris was in shock and to this day doesn't remember what happened after that. Keith tells how he picked up their daughter from her hospital bed to take her to the morgue. He pushed his wife, who then was holding Kelly, down to the morgue in a wheelchair because she couldn't walk. She was too upset.

"Picking Kelly's casket out was the hardest thing I ever did," Keith says. The couple agreed on a white one.

"I picked out a silver cross with Jesus on it and took it and placed it in her hand," Keith says. "I told the undertaker I wanted it in her hand for all eternity."

"She looked just like she was sleeping, with her little bonnet on her head," Doris said."

"She was buried in Babyland, a burial ground for babies under the age of three. It doesn't matter how old the child is that you lose," Keith said, "those feelings are always there."

Doris says that their initial response was that, "We didn't talk about it much."

"We were like two ships that passed in the night," Keith says. "We went to work and did what we had to do to get through our lives."

"And sometimes," Doris said through tears, "We would sit at the table and cry."

"We had a wake for Kelly at our house and I couldn't face the people," Keith says. "Everybody's laughing and talking and here I was, having lost my child. I just couldn't participate. I'd rather have fought a war than lose my child."

Keith went on to say how romance was not a part of their lives at the time because of their grief. After about four or five months they thought about adopting because they were afraid that they would pass the Werdnig-Hoffman disease onto another child of their own. When that didn't work out, they decided to have another child. Their son Keith was born later, without the disease. He was an active baby and his mother remembers saying, "Thank you, God. Thank you, God."

However, both Keith and Doris were still grieving.

The couple found that laughter with their family and friends was helpful to make them feel better about their loss. "We went out with friends and got out as much as possible," Keith said. Doris agreed. "Going out to dances, movies, and car shows helped, too," she says. "Sometimes on the weekends we would go to my parents and I would help my mother and Keith would help my dad. In the evenings, we'd go visit friends. If you have a good support team around you, it helps."

"You never, never, never get over it," Keith says. "You can listen to every person on television and in this field, and they don't know what they're talking about. For the first couple of months, we didn't talk. We'd both be at the table with no conversation passing between us. It was quiet and the silence was deafening. You could sense something was wrong."

"We loved each other and were in it for the long haul from day one together but we just didn't talk that much then," Doris says. "Instead of saying something to demean each other or blame each other, we didn't talk. A lot of couples when they lose a child, they separate. I guess they don't have that closeness or tie to get through it and be there for each other. Even though we didn't talk much after Kelly passed, maybe that's what we needed to do to get through it. To make sure that whatever came out of our mouths wouldn't hurt each other."

"At that particular time, when Kelly passed," Keith says, "we could have made fantastic alcoholics, if we would have wanted to. But we didn't." Doris agreed. "A lot of people climb into the bottle when a tragedy like that happens. But you have got to go on."

Were there things they did that made them feel worse? "Going to the cemetery often because we weren't ready to say goodbye," Doris says. "We didn't have her for a long period of time."

"That was hurtful," Keith says. "For awhile there, we were going there almost daily. And I think that was just hurtful to everybody involved."

"It was but we just weren't ready to let go," Doris says. "We knew what had happened and everything we went through but we just weren't ready. Then we tried to spend time with our families and friends which helped."

"One day, we went to go see Kelly's grave and I said to Doris, 'you know, there's about a hundred other babies here. Where are their parents?' We came to the same conclusion that we didn't have to be there every day. She's somewhere else now with somebody else."

"We kept her pictures up at first and then after awhile we put them away because, as our son got older," Doris says, "his friends began to ask questions and I didn't want him to have to answer those questions with his friends."

People said and did things that did help. "My aunt, Kelly's Godmother, called just about every week and told me that where Kelly is now, she is completely healed," Doris says. "She said to remember not the sadness but that she is not suffering, no pain, she's breathing, she's walking and she will be fine. And then nuns said a Prayer for the Innocents for Kelly. It's so unfair. She just didn't have a chance."

"I think the saddest words you'll ever hear," Keith says, "Is what might have been. You have to get away from things like, 'if she'd have lived.' That is hurtful. You can't think things like, "she would have been a mother by now or she would have been a doctor.' "

"I can't go there," Doris says.

Did anybody do or say anything at all that didn't help? "After Kelly passed," Doris says, "Someone said to me, 'don't worry about getting a baby room ready for your next one until you know everything is ok.' That really hurt."

"Someone told me," Keith says, "'God works in mysterious ways.' I didn't like that much."

What role did their faith play? "It helped," Doris says. Keith agreed. "You start thinking, if Jesus can get nailed on the cross, have a sword stuck in his side and the soldiers gamble for his clothes, then I can get through this."

"They say time heals," Doris says.

"You can't blame God for it," Keith says. "If Kelly would have lived, that would have been hell because of all the physical needs she would have had. My Uncle said that it is a blessing in disguise because of that."

"There were times when we thought we should have done more but we know now that is not true," Keith said. "Yes. We put our faith in the doctors that were caring for her, the scientists who were testing the biopsy, and the Almighty," Doris says. "And that's all we had to go on and then we had our faith in each other to keep us together because there are so many people who can't handle that and they split because each one is blaming the other. Maybe we did blame each other but we didn't say it because we knew it would be hurtful because we were still grieving."

Neither Doris nor Keith went for grief counseling. "We would talk about it with friends," Keith says. "Sometimes it's easier to talk with somebody outside the family," Doris says.

What do they do today to help? "We dedicated our front yard to Kelly and called it 'Kelly's Park,'" Doris says. "There's a bench and a fountain there and a statue that represents a friend for Kelly. That helps us."

"Sometimes I go out there and talk to her," Keith says.

When Doris and Keith think of their daughter now, they think of her as she was when she passed except that now they see her as a healthy child. "That helps me to know that she's one of God's little angels," Doris says.

How was grieving for Kelly different from grieving for others? "Because she was ours," Keith said. "The grief for something that came out of you is altogether different."

"She was something we made out of love," Doris says.

Neither Keith nor Doris have any regrets about the way that they grieved.

What did they learn from Kelly's passing? "How precious little ones are," Doris says. "There is so much neglect and abuse for the little ones coming into this world."

For people who are reading this book Keith says, "Be patient with yourself. Don't blame yourself. Talk to people about it. Go to church and talk to the minister. Don't blame God for what happens."

Doris says, "Don't blame God. He is there to help. As time goes on, your perspective on it changes. You just keep going on with your life or else you die a little inside." She cried when trying to say all of this.

According to Doris and Keith, their daughter was brilliant, always smiling, precious, rarely cried, and was a happy baby who was a perfect little angel.

Frankie Everton Haywood
Age - 49
1/29/1956 to 12/24/2005

~

Bonita (Sentis) Glenda Haywood
Age - 53
2/13/1954 to 12/28/2007

*As told by: John and Rubina Haywood,
Frankie's and Sentis's parents.*

Most of the stories in this book deal with the loss of one child. Not so with John and Rubina Haywood, American citizens formerly of British Guiana. They suffered the loss of both their son and a daughter, Frankie and Sentis, within the space of two years and four days.

During the interview, Rubina did most of the talking with John coming out only for the last twenty minutes as it is still too difficult for him to discuss the loss of his children.

"Our kids should bury us," Rubina says. "And it is so difficult when we have to bury them. My heart was ripped out of place that morning when my daughter died. Our daughter usually came three days before Christmas but this time she came the night before Christmas and I was a little upset. But since it was Christmas I didn't want to quarrel. She finally came. When she finally entered the driveway, I said to John, 'get the camera out and take her photo as soon as she gets in the driveway.' As soon as they came in here, I said, 'come on, let's hold hands and pray. I usually do that when they are leaving.

Never did that when they arrive. We stood there and we held hands and we prayed. I said 'ok, have a seat at the table' and I go to get the food.

After she died, when I called the ambulance and they took her out and as I got to the hospital, they pronounced her. So I called home. It's a good thing I'm a believer in Christ because if I didn't believe in God, I don't know how I'd do it. Someone I know used to say, 'If you believe in God, you would not fly in the face of the almighty because you believe and his strength is gonna take you through. The way that my daughter died was a blessing, though. A beautiful way to go. No lingering and no pain. Even though I'm sorry that my daughter died, when I consider things I say, 'Thank you God, you're an awesome God. It could have been worse.'

The year Frankie died we were all going to go down to Miami to spend Christmas with Sentis. He died the day before Christmas."

Frankie had been in the Air Force where he learned to repair cars. His death came when he was shot by the police during an incident.

"His case was pathetic," Rubina says. "We hired a private investigator from Atlanta, Georgia to find the facts of his death because we wanted closure. That's how we knew what really happened. I don't like the circumstances of my son dying but I'm contented to know he did not linger and suffer. I told my husband, God took him out of this world. He didn't have any pain. He didn't have to go to the hospital.' You still think of it but after a number of years you get over it.

God gives you the strength to go on. I keep praying. He has a nice twenty-four-year-old son who stays in touch with us."

How did they respond initially to his passing? "It's like shock," Rubina says. "It's like something like a dream. You don't believe that it's reality that really happened. I have my crying days. I go into the bathroom and I say, 'Father God, give me the strength, please, please.' When I cried for my son I used to go into the garage, too, close the door and say, 'Lord, please Jesus help me. How can you do this to me?' But you know I'm a strong person.

The day he died, I went to church. I heard the news after coming home from church. I had never worn black to church but that Sunday morning, I wore black shoes, a black hat, and a black dress. After church, the doorbell rang and there were two police, coming to tell me the news."

"Oh my God," Rubina says. "I said, 'no wonder he didn't come home last night.' I was in shock."

After time went on, the grieving process for both Frankie and Sentis unfolded about the same way for Rubina. "I start thinking about the good things, the happy things and how we would laugh. He called his father 'Amigo' and that made us laugh. I think about the times I could talk to Frankie no matter what it was about. He was never mad. I could tell him the worst thing and when he come back home, you wouldn't know I had been upset with him when he left."

What helped ease her burden? 'There were so many things. I try to remember the good times all the time.

My son loved to eat and was always in the refrigerator looking for something to eat. It was funny. And Sentis, she would always call to see what was going on with her father. She loved her father. She was so caring. There were so many nice things she did, always giving us money for something we need. She has a son who is just like her."

What made her feel worse? "Seeing my daughter lying on the bed there, helpless. I try not to remember it. And I try not to remember that morning when I wore black to church and those two cops were knocking on my door."

Does having their deceased childrens' pictures out bother them? "It doesn't bother me,' Rubina says. "But I don't look at them often. You must try to remember the good things. Whenever I think about sad things, it gets me down. But once I remember the good things, it's ok."

Rubina went to the bedroom and brought back a dress that she had made for Sentis. "That brought back such beautiful memories when I saw that."

After John Haywood joined us, we got his point of view on some of the topics.

Were there things that people said to you that didn't help? "It helped me when people talked about it the first week or two after the deaths. But I didn't like to hear about it after that," Rubina says. "I would get teary, emotional, and want to cry."

"I just want to forget it," John says.

What role did their faith play in the grieving process? "Great. Great. Because of believing in God, I know that everything happens for a reason. I know that from believing in God we have a timeline to live and to die and I know that some of us are gonna go early and some of us are gonna go later."

"God don't make mistakes," John said. "He called him home for a reason."

Did they attend any grief counseling? They both said no. "My husband and I have been married 55 years," Rubina says. "We are so entwined and close to each other that we held onto each other and that gave us the strength. Along with putting God first. We didn't stay in this house and mope and mope and mope. We didn't do it. God knows better and it could have been worse."

"After his death and we went up and arranged for the funeral. On the way back we stopped at the doctors and got some medicine to take to help," John says. "People bawl and we didn't have to. We were normal because of it."

"After the funeral, about a week later, we didn't need it," Rubina says.

Do they have any regrets about the grieving process? "I am happy for the way we did it," Rubina says.

Is there anything at all that you learned from these two difficult experiences?

"I have learned that you should tell others how much you appreciate them and how much you love them," Rubina says. "Because you don't know when you're not going to have them around."

"What I always look back and remember," John says, "At 3 o'clock in the morning, Sentis was here with a friend, making steaks, playing music. They came into our room and invited us to come out and have steaks with them and play dominoes. I should have gone. Because at 8 o'clock in the morning, I went to her room and she was dead from a massive heart attack. I should have gone at 3 a.m. and had a piece of steak with her. I always remember that. And every time I go into that room where she died, I remember finding her there."

Is there anything else that you think a reader might want to read about what happened to you? "I would say that because of our belief in God, we weren't mad because my two kids died," Rubina said. "I was more in shock. But, because of my belief in God I wasn't mad about it because I felt that the dear Lord knows what is best. I was not happy that my son was shot, but I would have been more hurt if my son was in a fight and been shot and caused it. I would have been hurt to know that he died like that. I would like other parents to know that you should enjoy every moment that the dear Lord gives you of your children. Try not to remember the wrongs that they did but try to remember the pleasant things that they did in their lives. That is what I'm doing."

John says, "I think about how Frankie was very athletic, was good in games. He was a very handy guy."

The parents describe Frankie as athletic, a trumpet player, jovial, loved to laugh, a knowledgeable mechanic, healthy, and he loved his niece Shua.

Sentis, according to her parents, was generous, intelligent, made strong friendships, and was loving. She didn't know she was going to die but she lived her life by giving to others.

Sentis's car has never been moved from the spot of her parent's driveway where she parked it on the day that she died.

John (Johnny) Alexander Bishop
2 ½ Years Old
12/7/1969 to 05/14/1972 (Mother's Day)

As told by: Barbara Towers, Johnny's mother.

A happy toddler, Johnny was sick a lot as a child with bronchitis and pneumonia but his parents did not know that he had a heart condition until the day he passed. His mother would tell the doctors during his checkups that he seemed to be having trouble breathing but, according to his mother, the doctors didn't think there was anything wrong with him. Later, his doctor would say that, because of his heart condition, if Johnny had not been delivered Cesarean, he would not have survived birth through the birth canal.

"So, in a way, having the Cesarean section was a blessing for me because I had those years with this great little boy and I got to know his personality," Barbara says.

According to Barbara, Johnny was outside playing the day before he died, running around, and eating his usual meals. "He was just a great little boy and he played like a normal kid and I guess in a way that was good because I wasn't hovering over him. He got to live his life," Barb says.

"I went to get him up the next morning and his hands, tops of his feet, and his face were swollen, I thought it was some kind of allergic reaction to something. I couldn't get him to move. I called the ambulance and I think he died when we got him into the ambulance. He was gone. The doctors said his cardiac arteries were both on the one side so the heart was never pumping right. The autopsy results showed an enlarged heart and enlarged liver.

I guess if you know ahead of time that something is wrong with your child, it is a little easier in some respects. At least you know what you are dealing with and have time to do some grieving and some preparation. I was in so much shock that I don't know what happened after that because they numbed me right away. You know, I just couldn't imagine what happened. I wondered what I could have done differently. I took him to all his doctor's appointments.

So when my second son was born, panic set in. I had a wonderful set of pediatricians with him. They knew my history so they looked him over real close. Now, babies that have these kinds of problems like Johnny have a better chance because they have tests that pick up things. Even with heart surgery, I'm sure the survival rate is a lot higher than back in 1972.

You never have an answer as to why these things happen and I've had to look at it differently once I got over the horrible part of it and was in reality. You have to look at it as you had a blessing for 2 ½ years. I don't know that you get over it but, I can get through his birthday and Christmas a lot better now. Mother's Day is still pretty tough but he's never out of my mind. And now, with my second son Chris, and Chris's son both looking so much like Johnny, it's almost like a gift. It's like a second chance."

Initially, when Barb realized that her son Johnny was dead, she went into shock. The doctors immediately gave her some meds to help her to cope.

The grieving process was put on hold for Barb while she was working for a pharmaceutical company in Baltimore. "I just didn't deal with it," she says. "And I couldn't talk to my husband and the church did nothing to help us. So, there was no support. I just kept it inside. I never really grieved until after I was divorced in 1987 from Johnny's father. Chris went to live with his father and then there was all that loss to face. I had to move out of my house. I was working on my master's degree also which was more pressure.

In 1988, after about 16 years, it caught up with me. I ended up needing someone to talk to and release the hurt and anger I had so that I might move on. Everything hit me all at once. I crashed. Up until then, nothing fazed me. I just kept going and going and going. And then when it hit, my whole system crashed. I didn't know why I was even around because I didn't have my sons. I had a wonderful counselor who made me go to an inpatient unit to help me deal with everything. The whole thing was pretty bad. Even my grandparents whom I loved had already passed away. I guess everything just piled up and I couldn't work on it anymore. I think that all that work overload had to do with filling those empty hours that I spent with my son Chris. He was my entire life by then."

"I think sometimes when you grieve, you need someone to talk to," Barb says. "I mean, you think you can go to your pastor to talk but where I attended church, that was not possible. I encourage people who are going through this to start grieving in whatever shape or form it takes. If you want to cry everyday for fifteen or twenty minutes, go ahead. Whatever it takes. Do not harbor it because sooner or later it's going to come at you in another way. If you don't talk about it, it's gonna get you. People who haven't been through it don't get that."

There were things that Barb was doing which helped her feel better. "I had a good job with co-workers that were good to work with. It helped. I didn't really have a whole lot of time to think about other things. I was working and doing my Master's program and that took up all my time."

Things that made her feel worse? "I think when I started to dwell on the past and think that maybe Johnny's death was a punishment," Barb says. "I tried not to do that a whole lot. I don't think you realize the impact that a child's loss has on you."

Barb has examples of things that people said that did not help her. "I had people say, 'It was God's timing.' That didn't sit well with me. Another one said, 'Well you must not have taken him to enough doctors.' That hurt. I had one lady tell me it was time to get over it. I thought maybe she should have been in my shoes to know. I don't remember anyone saying to me, 'would you like to talk about it?' That would have helped."

There were some things that people did that helped. "I had some nice wonderful friends at work and they would take me to lunch or shopping, especially on Johnny's birthday. I had friends along the way who would talk about it with me and then we would do something fun. You have to do that—talk about it. "

Barb did not attend any grief counseling after her son passed until 1988. "Johnny's always on my mind—wondering if he had lived—what would he be like?"

Grieving for her son was different from grieving for anyone else she knew who had passed. This experience was much harder and she has never forgotten him. Barb kept John's photos out for awhile but since they moved, she now keeps one on the wall and one in her wallet.

Barb's regrets about how she grieved revolve around her inability to grieve soon after Johnny passed. "I carried all that inside of me for years," Barb says. "I was never able to share it with others. Now, I wish I could have."

What did she learn from the experience? "The fact that my faith was still there," Barb says. "Without that, I wouldn't have made it."

Barb has some advice for other parents who have lost a child. "Stay involved with people and talk about it. Find something you enjoy doing and get involved doing it. Don't wait years to grieve," she says. "Allow time for yourself to grieve. You must get the grief out. Then it's time to go on with life. When your child is gone, they're gone. There's nothing more that you can do and you have to go on. You are not without pain but you go on."

Barb describes Johnny as a good boy, a cuddly baby with a sweet disposition. She says he loved music, books, and loved being read to.

Mary "Chris" Szuba
Age - 51
10/26/1956 to 11/29/2007

As told by: Sally Fairchild, Chris's mother

Chris Szuba passed away November 29, 2007 after a battle with ovarian cancer which was discovered in March of the same year. Chris's symptoms were fatigue, bloating, and lower back pain. Sally says, "I've always believed that there are no coincidences. Everything happens for a reason. Her symptoms could be a number of problems and, as her physician suspected gall bladder, they needed an MRI. It not only showed an ailing gall bladder, but an abdomen full of cancer. A CA125 blood test confirmed cancer and Chris was immediately sent to Orlando to begin her journey. Chris's attitude was positive and she enjoyed remission that summer long enough to vacation in Wisconsin with her three siblings and families. But the cancer and complications returned. The day we lost her, we had a glimmer of hope that she could beat it again. When I left about 7 p.m. I tried to believe that the next day would be better, in spite of her pain."

Chris passed away at her home in the arms of her husband, Tom. That evening, about 9:30 p.m., Sally was at home when Tom called to tell her of her daughter's passing. She refused the offer of a ride and drove over to be with the family.

Sally believed she had to be strong for her grandchildren. "I wasn't really tearful because I felt I had to be strong," Sally says. "I still feel that way but it does sometimes bring me to tears. I've always been strong, maybe too stoic.

My ongoing grieving process was mostly gratitude for having had her for 51 years, and my deep gratitude that Chris was no longer in such excruciating pain," Sally says. "Even the years that I was busy with my life and so was she, we were aware of how much we loved each other. With the advent of her two precious children we were again in each others lives. Both parents worked and I had the privilege of being the baby sitter. A year or two before she died, I started telling her I loved her at each parting. I'm glad for that. It's better for both of you if you say just that. I was always grateful that Chris had learned to say that before she died."

Were there things that Sally was doing that made her feel better? "I was more in shock than anything. When anything bad happens to me, I've been like an observer ever since. I observe myself and it doesn't seem quite as bad."

What made Sally feel worse? "Anything and everything," Sally says. "And when the funeral home called to pick up Chris' ashes, I went for them and then I wondered, 'what am I doing?' It didn't give me any finality, it just needed to be done. The other thing is that I wasn't able to help Chris more. She was in such pain. My arthritis disallowed my helping as I wanted to as Chris was worrying about my pain. At least I could be there all day. Neither of us wanted her to be alone." Another thing that bothered her was when Sally was watching television and some kid yelled 'mom' on the tv show. To her it sounded just like Chris.

"When I picture Chris now, I picture her doing something, anything, because she was always busy," Sally says. "For me she's not really gone," Sally says. "She's still with us."

Sally didn't remember anybody saying something that hurt her grieving.

Were there things that people said that helped? "Chris's daughter said, 'Gram, I just want you to know that mom knew how much you loved her. And I want you to know how much she loved you.' That was the best thing of everything."

Did Sally's faith play a role in the grieving process? "Everything. I feel so sorry for people who have a loss of that magnitude and don't have a place to go. I feel that help from my faith all the time. I'm always connected to my faith and I know that I will see Chris again in heaven."

Sally attended Compassionate Friends, a group for parents who have lost a child. It has been a source of comfort for her because, "Everyone there understands," Sally says. "It's a different kind of grief, losing a child. Even different than losing your mother.

I cope now, just by taking one day at a time and

living the serenity prayer," Sally says. "I don't look to tomorrow. I don't have tomorrow yet. I try to be the best I can be today. Sometimes I think I'm numb all the time."

Sally says she doesn't have any regrets with how she dealt with the grieving process but she did learn things from her loss. "I wish I had started saying, 'I love you,' earlier than I did," Sally says. "I wasn't sure if I had tomorrow so I realized that my family needed to hear it now."

What would Sally want readers to know? "I'd say to anybody, they should live one day at a time. I have been at peace since I learned to do that. If I had one wish it would be that the insurance companies would change their policy of not paying for the CA125 blood test that confirms cancer. They say it's too expensive. I'd say it's a lot cheaper than paying all the costs of treatment. And think of the lives we could save with early detection."

Linda M. Hosburgh
Age - 32
6/8/1957 to 9/20/1989

As told by: Betty Gilligan, Linda's mother

Linda had five sisters and brothers who loved her very much. She was a Cardiac Intensive Care Nurse who spent her professional life helping others, including helping as a volunteer paramedic and ambulance driver.

While in a state of depression, Linda committed suicide through the use of a firearm after an unsuccessful previous attempt with pills. "She had been fighting depression for ten or twelve years, on again, off again," Betty says. "Looking back I now believe that she was probably Bi-Polar."

When Linda was missing after being released from the hospital due to her attempted suicide with pills, her mother drove all over town searching for her and made phone calls to locate her, all without success. Soon after she completed her search, a policeman came to Betty's home to tell her that her daughter had been found dead that afternoon.

"I screamed, and screamed and screamed and screamed at the top of my lungs. One of my other daughters, Debra, came over to me and I stopped screaming because she was blaming herself for Linda's death. I told her not to blame herself because Linda would have found a way. I had to stop screaming because I realized I was traumatizing Debra. So I stopped.

Linda wanted to make sure this time that it would be instant death," Betty says, "because the pills didn't work the first time. She was so tired of being depressed that she wanted to get out of life and that's what she wanted to do. I can hardly look at a tv program now when they show someone who is going to commit suicide with a gun.

What comforts me is that I know now she is at peace. For ten or twelve years she suffered from depression. She's now at peace. I put that on her stone next to her date of death. A lot of people don't understand what depression can do to you."

How did the grieving process unfold after the initial screaming? "I had many sleepless nights for many months," Betty says. "Just reliving everything surrounding Linda's death. The pills, the rush to the ER, the hospitalization, her release from the hospital, not being able to find her the next day and then the police that afternoon telling me she had died. Then the funeral arrangements, the viewing and funeral. It was like a tape in my head playing over and over again. It would hit me again sometimes and I would be crying. What brought me out of the crying spell is that I would picture Linda shaking her finger at me from Heaven saying, 'Mother, stop crying. Life is for the living. I'm at peace. Get on with life. I'm fine.' And that would bring me back. She was too full of life when she wasn't depressed. And she's at peace now. She's out of her suffering. I was comforted in the idea of her having some peace. And I still miss her. You don't stop missing them. The pain gets easier. I had read somewhere how losing a child is like losing a limb. At first the pain is intense. As the wound heals, it throbs. Then in time, you still have some pain but then the wound heals. You are always aware that the limb is missing. That is exactly what it is. The intense pain is gone but you are always aware that it's missing."

What did Betty do that helped ease her grief? "I worked. I went back to work two weeks after Linda's death and that helped. You need to get back into life. My kids and I will always talk about Linda. About the funny things she did. We have some nice memories about her."

Betty couldn't remember anything that she did that made her feel worse. "I just wish I would have picked up more on her illness. I did say, 'if only,' but generally I try to keep a more positive frame of mind."

Pictures of Linda when she graduated from high school and also when she graduated from nursing school adorn Betty's walls. A beautiful brunette smiles out from the photos.

There were some things that people said after Linda passed that did not help. "One thing I remember was when I went to the hospital where Linda worked, to the office after Linda died, and someone asked me if I had other children. And I said, 'yes, I have five others.' That person said, 'Oh good, you have other children.' What difference does it make that I have other children? Like having the other children is going to lessen the pain of Linda's death. What a stupid thing to say. That was the only negative thing that I remember."

There were things that helped Betty. "One of the things that gave me great comfort was the large number of people that came to Linda's funeral. Her friends and relatives flew in from out of state. The ambulance squad flew their flag at half-staff for a month and had a sign out front showing it was in Linda's memory. That gave me comfort."

Faith played a large role in Betty's grieving. "What do people do when they don't have faith or a belief in a higher power?" Betty says. "I know that God takes people in His time. It was her time. God knew that she couldn't go on any longer. The priest came to my house that day and talked to me a little bit. Once, during the Thanksgiving season when I went to church, during the sermon, the priest was talking about 'the empty chair at the Thanksgiving table.' I broke down crying because I knew there was going to be an empty chair at my home. Every time he said it, it broke my heart. You have to cry. Crying releases all the pent-up grief. You try to hold it down and go on with life but you have to let it out. It's like a cleansing. Thank you, God. There are so many other things to be thankful for and you've got to really dwell on what is good in life, not the bad."

Did Betty attend grief counseling? "I joined the grief and bereavement group at church which was once a week. Most of the people there had lost husbands and it was different from my situation. I also joined another group for several months. I stopped going to that one because everyone was stuck in their grief. I tried to talk hopeful so that it would give them an idea of how to get out of their doldrums. I would go back the next month and nothing positive was happening. It was just bringing me down so I quit going. I was doing well and wanted to help them but they were all stuck."

How does Betty handle her grief now? "I think of her everyday. Sometimes I picture her coming to visit me on her way to work or after work when she'd stop by for a chat. I think of the good times she had with all her traveling. And when the family gets together, we talk about Linda. Nobody is afraid to mention her name."

"I've never been angry at God and I've never been

angry at Linda, either," Betty says. "Thy will be done, and all things work together for good."

One thing that Betty learned is that a person needs a will with the beneficiaries that you want, because you never know what is going to happen. It's possible that your estate will go where you would not want it to go.

What would Betty want others who are grieving for a child to know? "Life is for the living," Betty says. "As much as you grieve for your child, life is for the living and you cannot die within yourself just because your child dies. You still have to keep on living until it's your time. Especially if you have other children. If you grieve so much that the other children are forgotten, you have to remember that you have other family members who depend on you. You still have to keep that emotional and physical connection with your other children because they are grieving, too."

David
Age - 30
7/31/1957 to 2/13/1988

As told by: David's mother

David was a bright young man who died from AIDS after a two-year illness. After finding out about his being sick, his parents took him to Washington D.C. on a family trip. After that, he was in and out of the hospital and, as his quality of life deteriorated, he decided not to treat his latest infection.

His parents were with him a lot at the hospital where David chose not to take in nourishment, instead taking in just water. David was aware of everything throughout that time while his family and sisters took turns taking care of him. Despite the AIDS diagnosis at a time when it was a fairly new disease, the family educated themselves about the illness and took care of him.

His mother's initial response to David's death was different from his father's. David's father was so distraught, he could not come back into the hospital room when it was evident his son was dying. David vomited a lot of fluid during his last minutes which was distressing to his mother and sister who were there. "We comforted him and said our goodbyes and went home," his mother says. "After I got home, I realized I was crying and upset and I had a headache and was sick to my stomach. I've stopped crying at all sad events, even at my husband's death. I know I must function and cannot do so if I feel ill."

The grieving process for David included relief that he wasn't suffering anymore. "That was good," she says. "You think of things you should have said and done but we said quite a bit as it was. We had time to think about it. When they're sick for awhile, you have time to think about the goodbyes. And back then, people didn't understand much about AIDS."

There were some things that people said and did that were not helpful for David's mother. "There were people who came to our home and wouldn't use the bathroom," she says. "I could tell that it was because our son had AIDS. And there were some relatives and other people who never did go to see him. You kind of remember those things. And yet, there were other relatives who informed themselves about AIDS and they went to see him. Everybody handled it differently. Even amongst the nurses, some would gown up to go in to his room even when they didn't have to. The doctors told them they didn't have to do that and some realized he was a gay man and they didn't like that too much. I remember at David's service, people were silent about him. I felt bad about that. They didn't know what to say. Some people thought that gay people deserved AIDS because the country kind of looked at it that way at that time. We did have a good support group that I attended and we still keep in touch."

In the support group that David's mother attended, there were people who had gone through what she was experiencing and they knew how she was feeling. She gives much credit to the leader of the group saying, "Without her, we would have been lost."

What things that she was doing made her feel better? "Keeping in contact with the people in the support group helped. Speaking up for the gay community has helped too. I used to hear things said about them, putting them down, and I wouldn't say anything. Now I speak up and say, 'have you really thought about it? You're putting these people down and you don't really know them. You don't understand.' I remember years ago I didn't want to start any conflict but I don't do that anymore. I speak up. And I've made good friends through all of this too. There are two gay men, one of whom was in the support group, who are so good to me. Especially after my husband passed away. They do things here at my home that need done or they ask if I need anything. That has been something good that has come of this."

When asked if faith played a role in her grieving, David's mother said, "Somewhat. We had a wonderful minister who came to see my son a lot. I'm not one who has to be in church all the time but the spirit is within you and helps you all the time." That comforts her.

When her husband was alive it was easier for her to deal with her son's death. However, now she keeps busy with a friend who had lost his wife. "He comes to my home twice a week and enjoys my cooking," she says. "So I have somebody to eat with. We enjoy each other's company, go for a ride together and sometimes have coffee together. And he helps sometimes to fix something here at my home. It helps."

Grieving for her son was different from any other grieving that David's mother experienced. "I think in my grieving I thought to myself, 'what could I have done differently when I raised David?' And I still wonder. I wish I had been a little more educated as he was growing up so I could have helped him more. I think I could have shown more understanding, too. Although I've found mothers accept a gay son more than fathers do. It would help if fathers would feel more compassion. It's not easy to be different. Who would choose that?"

David's mother believes she has learned some things from her son's passing. "I learned to be more compassionate and sensitive to other people. Especially being sensitive to those who grieve for their children. I also believe that young people should be reminded of things that can happen to them in their lives if they aren't careful."

"When I said to David that he had a hard life (being gay)," she says, "he said, 'No. I had a wonderful life.' That made me feel good."

Howard Dewey Crandall, II
Age - 21
8/3/1947 to 9/1968

As told by: Jean Crandall, Howard's mother

As a teenager, Howard worked closely with his mother in the office of his father, a medical doctor. His mother described Howard as being her right-hand man there, taking on responsibilities such as doing bank deposits and carrying them out in a mature manner. With a genius level I.Q., Howard had a bright future ahead of him but a congenital condition changed what was to be. The 6' 4" handsome young man's weight dropped to less than 150 lbs and he passed away at the age of 21 from kidney failure, despite having been on dialysis.

"I had grieved from the time he was four years old," Jean says. That was when the family realized the seriousness of Howard's condition.

Together, the family of seven traveled thousands of miles together, camping and driving to provide adventures and experiences for them while Howard was able to participate.

After Howard passed, Jean wasn't always able to let her feelings show. Some of the patients who came to her husband's office for treatment would express their condolences, but Jean rarely broke down there. "I could grieve but I couldn't get into it," Jean says. Part of it she attributes to the time period and part of it to Yankee stoicism. "Once in awhile, a patient and I would cry together," Jean says, "but basically, you had to keep going. I couldn't grieve in front of them."

Jean's husband, a family practice physician, felt guilty that he couldn't save their son. Frustrated and depressed, he sat next to their son's casket where it was placed in the funeral home, holding his hand and grieving. The beginning of his healing came later when he began to ride Howard's motorcycle with Jean.

Jean felt she had to be strong for her husband and the rest of the family but the grieving has not really ended for her. "It just comes up once in awhile," she says.

Was there anything that Jean did that made her feel better? "Actually, when we had Thanksgiving and Christmas and we had 30 or 40 people here, that made everybody feel better. The entertaining was helpful."

What made her feel worse? "Basically when patients and friends would come in to the office and we'd talk and cry. A lot of those patients were going through the same thing with a spouse, a child, or a grandchild. I realize now that I had a long grieving process because some of the patients only came in once a year and that would be the only time I saw them." So when they came in for their appointment, even though it was months or even a year later, they would express their condolences.

What did people say that didn't help her grief? "There were one or two people who irritated me," Jean says. "One of them said, 'Oh, he's in a better place.' But that's not helpful when they say that. You have to be patient with people."

There were things that people said that helped but there was nothing specific that Jean could cite.

Jean claims that faith and patience got her through many things. Sometimes when she had faced the difficulties of illness and death, she would go to bed, pray, and then say, "I have to go to sleep now, Jesus."

Jean didn't attend grief counseling. Instead, she and her husband were the ones whom others contacted for assistance with their grief.

When asked if there is anything she would want readers to know, Jean says, "My husband always said, 'Hang loose.' " Jean also advises the readers not to expect the pain to go away. "The sadness is always with you," she says. "In this culture, we don't allow people the time and space to grieve. If they won't allow it for you, give it to yourself. You don't have to go out and socialize. You don't have to act like it's okay for everyone else. Everybody has to grieve."

Donnis "Donnie" Helms
Age - 28
8/4/1971 to 10/12/2000

As told by: Judy Kuhns, Donnie's mother

Donnie Helms was a young father who loved doing carpentry. He passed away in the year 2000 at the age of 28 from chronic meningitis. Despite knowing he has died, his mother Judy still waits every Mother's Day to receive a phone call from her beloved younger son.

"I got a phone call one night about 11:30 or 12 midnight telling me that I needed to get to a hospital in Sebring, that my son was real sick and they didn't know if he was going to make it through the night," Judy says. "I knew he had pneumonia because I had just been there to see him a couple of days earlier, but didn't think he was near death."

The hospital informed Judy that her son had a change for the worse and that he was in ICU, so Judy and her husband went to see him at the hospital. That was in December, 1999, right after Christmas. He recovered a little, was discharged, but continued to have times when he was sick and needed hospitalization. By April of the next year, Donnie was blind and eventually lost his hearing. He was diagnosed with chronic meningitis. Donnie's deteriorating illness was a shock to his mother.

There were times when Donnie had seizures because of the intense pain. "I remember a time when he was so sick and I was holding his head and I said, 'why you?' Donnie said, 'why not?' I thought, what a man, and wondered if I would be saying something like that if it was me. I asked God, 'Why my son? Where are you, God? Where are you?'

The wonderful thing that I found out one time when I was screaming at God and asking him, 'Where are you?' I said, 'don't you see, God,' I prayed for people, I had helped people and this is not their son. This is my son. Don't you know how I feel?' And just like that, I couldn't see God, but I knew he was there, and he said, 'Yes, I know just how you feel. You know, my son died, too. He died a very cruel, hard death and he was in a lot of pain. My son died so that your son can live.'" Judy admits she had never thought about it like that. "All I could say was, 'Thank you,' " she says.

A couple of weeks before her son died, Judy noticed a sweet smell in the room and when she got closer to Donnie's head, she realized it was coming from him. To her the smell was like that of a newborn baby. Judy thought at the time that when a person passes away, it is like when a child is born and enters a new world and that it is the same as when a person dies. They go on to another place.

The day that Donnie died, Judy had not been there to see him for a couple of days because she was sick with a bad cold and she didn't want to give it to him. "I walked into his room that morning, and just as I stepped into the doorway, I heard in my heart, 'Today, Donnie will be graced with grace. Today.' I didn't know what that meant but I knew that I felt the Lord's presence. I walked over and I looked at him and I knew."

"One thing the Lord told me is that before my son

was born, he was inside me and he couldn't see anything and you couldn't see in. But once he was born and he came out, he went through that birth canal, then I could hold him and love him and touch him. After the Lord told me that Donnie would be graced with grace, I walked over to where Donnie was lying in the hospital bed. When I looked at him, he couldn't see or hear and was very still. The Lord told me, 'He's in the birth canal. He's going to be birthed into heaven.' "

Later that day, Judy had a doctor's appointment which she kept. She returned later after she received a phone call from her older son telling her to get to the hospital immediately. Judy ran from the parking lot to the hospital room where family members were gathered at Donnie's bed.

"I went over to him and took him by the hand, and I took his face and I said, 'Donnie, Donnie, stop this. You stop this right now.' That was one time I said, 'Lord, I know you always know what you're doing, but do you know what you're doing this time?' "

"We are their mothers," Judy said. "When our children were little and they bumped their knee or something, we kissed it and made it better. This time I couldn't help him. That was so hard."

Judy took her son's hand and ran it all over her face so he would know that it was his momma with him. "He had a tear come down his face," Judy says. "Then another tear rolled down his face. I screamed at Donnie's dad. I said, 'Donnis, we don't have to let him go. We can call his spirit back into his body.' And his father said, 'No. Let him go, Judy, he has hurt so much.'

When I looked up, I saw the Lord's hands holding Donnie's head and I said, 'Please, no.' The Lord didn't say anything, he just looked at me and I knew I had to let him go. Donnie's heart beat two more beats and it stopped. They said, 'He's gone.' I said, 'I know he's gone.' I just went out of the room and sat down. Then started the crazy part that was me."

"The hardest part was looking at the hole in the ground where they were going to put my son at his funeral. I couldn't stand it. It's not supposed to be like that. We're supposed to go first. That's why I questioned the Lord. I said, 'I know you're supposed to know everything, but I don't know about this one.' And I still don't have the answer to that. But I don't dwell on this anymore. I knew that Donnie was spiritually ready to go when he died."

Judy remembers driving to work about two weeks later and not knowing how she got there. She cannot remember what she worked on but believes her friend did more of her work than she did. She doesn't remember a lot of it.

"One time a woman called me at work and was talking about her son. She said that she would rather her son was dead than in prison and I totally lost it," Judy says. "I said, 'No you don't,' and I totally went off on her. Then I retreated. I didn't clean my house. Why clean it? It doesn't matter. I still don't care.

I remember driving down to work one day and I remember now that I was totally lost. I didn't know where I was," Judy says. "One of the things I found out was, it's ok. It really is. I have a tendency now that when people come to me and they are telling me little trivial things, I don't care. I've lived through the absolutely biggest hurt in my life. I believe I could go through almost anything from now on except the loss of another child. I couldn't deal with that."

After Donnie died, Judy began to retreat from people. Especially the ones that she cared about. She felt numb and gained a lot of weight. She would go to work, come home, and sit down.

Judy says that she told her boss and coworkers that she would go back to work but she didn't want anyone asking her anything about her son because she couldn't deal with it. She still cannot remember all of what happened then because, according to her, she didn't know what she was doing.

"Three or four years after that, I still wouldn't meet with my children. I could not face them all together and Donnie not being there. And if I could keep them away from me and something happened to one of them, it wouldn't hurt so bad. That's the way I was thinking. I wouldn't have anything to do with them."

Judy's children and her husband were good to her, trying to help her get through her grief.

What did Judy do that made her feel worse? "When I retreated into myself. I needed to feel and I wasn't feeling anything. I would talk to people but it didn't matter what I said. I said whatever I wanted to because I didn't care what they thought. I didn't care for them. I went to church because I always went to church but if somebody wanted to say something to me I thought, 'Say what you want.' It didn't bother me because they couldn't touch me. I just retreated into myself. I stayed in the house, sitting on the sofa with the tv on all the time. I didn't want to wash clothes, do dishes or anything else because I didn't care. I hate to say it but it's true. The worse thing that I did was to push my children away."

What things did Judy do that made her feel better? "One of the things I've found that really helps me now is talking about him. And by being with my children and grandchildren."

What things did others do or say that made her feel worse? "I had someone a few years ago who told me that she was tired of me acting like I do. She said that I needed to get over it. She said 'Life goes on and it's hard to see someone get so fat and not care about themselves.' Then I felt as if everyone was laughing at me and I should try to lose weight."

What did others do that helped? "When a friend told me she was praying for me, that really helped. The prayers of others and my church really helped me."

Faith played a big role in Judy's grieving process. "It was everything," Judy says. "While driving to work I would talk to God and say, 'God, I can't bear this. I can't do this, my heart is hurting so bad. I can't deal with this anymore.' A lot of the times, I couldn't pray but would just talk to the Lord. I couldn't have made it through without him."

Judy never attended grief counseling and none was offered to her.

How does she cope now with her son's passing? "I stay very busy," she says. "What I do now is I like to help and love others. I bake cakes and prepare food for others. I'm finding that I want to do things for others that I have never done before. I'm healing."

Grieving for her child was different from other grieving that Judy did. "When my grandfather died, he was the first one really close to me who passed away. I missed him but he was old and I knew that old people are supposed to eventually die. When my grandmother died, I felt like she deserted me. It was different when they died than when Donnie died because they were expected to go. I gave birth to Donnie and he wasn't supposed to die. It's not supposed to happen. It's not supposed to be over for him."

The biggest regret that Judy has about how she dealt with her grief was pushing her family away and not interacting with her children and grandchildren.

The biggest thing that Judy says she learned from Donnie's death is that God is good. "Trust him," Judy says. "I never realized how you can really trust him. Because God is the only one who can fill that empty spot in your heart that comes when your child dies."

Judy wants other parents who are grieving to know this: "Trust God," she says. "He's trustworthy. Trust him to give you what you need. When you are numb and can't make any decisions or any sense out of anything, when you can't love anymore, when you can't feel and you think you should, when you are lost in your own home and feel very alone, when others are talking and you don't know what they have said, trust God and he will bring you through by his grace."

Steve Alan Brungard
Age - 3
5/1/1953 to 8/4/1956

As told by: Doris Williams, Steve's mother

Steve was an active little boy who was loving and sweet. He passed away in August of 1956 from what was then known as 'galloping cancer,' so called because it spread so fast. Though an octogenarian, his mother Doris remembers well her beautiful little boy, and the struggle they faced with this diagnosis.

"I knew Steve was not feeling well so I took him to the doctor who said there was nothing wrong with him. They gave him some medicine but every time I gave it to him, he screamed. We were living in Bloomsburg so I took him to his pediatrician in Williamsport, but they still couldn't find out what was wrong. The doctor knew there was something wrong, but he didn't know what. So, three months went by as we went to all different pediatricians in Williamsport and talked to as many people we could in town. We ended up taking him to a hospital in Philadelphia where they told us they would tell us what was wrong in twelve hours. And they did. But by that time the cancer was in his brain, two of his ribs were gone and his right kidney was gone. He lasted three months after that. At that time they didn't have many treatments for cancer."

"We had a wonderful minister at that time," Doris says. "He came to visit us every day while Steve was sick. He never missed a day. If he was late coming, Steve would notice it and say how the Pastor wasn't there yet. Steve really looked forward to those visits. Our pastor prayed with us, he cried and laughed with us and I couldn't have made it without him. He was my crutch to lean on. That pastor got us through it."

Doris spent the last three months holding her precious little boy. Steve passed away in his mother's arms at the Bloomsburg Hospital where he was admitted for morphine administration in the last few days of his life. "I was constantly at his side and so sad that he passed," Doris says, "but also relieved because he was in so much pain."

Doris grieved for Steve but, "I had two more sons aged seven and ten and they were completely ignored by me when Steve was sick because I gave him all my time," Doris says. "Thankfully, other family members and friends stepped in to take good care of them until I was able to do so again. So, after Steve passed we took the boys on a small trip. There was also a lot going on as my husband was transferred at his job to another town and we were forced to move about the same time. It was very tough but a good thing in a way because it occupied my time."

Doris was unable to remember anything that she did that either helped her grief or made her feel worse.

After Steve died, Doris gave birth to a daughter in 1958 and she remembers one woman telling her that she could never find another child to take Steve's place. "I never expected my daughter to take Steve's place," Doris says. "She was a real blessing and helped a lot with the grief."

Doris had an aunt who said something wonderful that did help her, though. "My aunt said to me 'You must have been special because you had such a special boy on loan to you from God for a short time.' That helped. I thank the Lord every night for loaning him to me."

Doris's faith played a big part in her grief. "It helped," Doris says. "It played a big part because I knew I was never alone. I'm counting on seeing Steve again."

Doris never attended any grief counseling nor was it offered to her.

How does Doris cope with her son's passing now? "I think about him every day," Doris says. "His pictures are still around the house." When she thinks of him now, she sees him as the tall, blonde, handsome man that she thought he would have been had he lived.

Doris's husband, who is deceased, was unable to face the grief of Steve's passing so he ignored it. Doris says he was a good dad and husband and was there for her but he couldn't face it.

Doris found that grieving for her son was deeper than the grieving she knew for others. "It's more intense because I was with him constantly," Doris says. "It was such a let-down and an alone feeling."

One thing that Doris says she learned from Steve's passing is, "Appreciate what you have. Do all you can for your children while you have them," Doris says. "Do it now so you don't have any regrets later. I'd give anything just to be able to hold him again."

Valerie Susan Derr
Age - 29 Weeks gestation
2/6/1963 to 2/6/1963

As told by: Kay Derr, Valerie's mother

Precious Valerie was born premature at the age of 29 weeks gestation. Kay was delighted to know she had a daughter. Valerie's pediatrician worked intently for nearly an hour to try to save her life but then told Kay that there was little hope for her baby's survival.

"Little Valerie Susan, our firstborn," Kay says, "Came into this world on February 6, 1963. We weren't really shocked that she was coming two months premature since problems in the pregnancy began at the second month. Twice, her delivery was averted with drugs, but this time I arrived at the hospital too late.

Seven months prior, I had purchased a baby rattle at Cain's Pharmacy with which to announce her coming to my husband. Now, as I was taken to a room, our baby struggled to breathe in the nursery. The nurse asked if I wanted her baptized and, since that was all I knew about 'going to heaven,' I said, 'Yes,' to which the nurse was given authority."

Kay's husband went with the funeral director, who had dressed Valerie in a little komona, and buried her. Kay could see the location of Valerie's resting place from her hospital window. "I went home empty-handed," Kay says, "And with a broken heart. When the song, 'Shake Me I Rattle, Squeeze Me I Cry' was popular, every time I heard it I ached for my little Valerie.

In those days, the parents of an ill-fated newborn

were not encouraged to see nor to hold their baby. To this day I regret that I wasn't there to comfort my baby while she struggled for her last breaths. Nor did I even get to see her. The regret of the loss of this experience has followed me throughout my lifetime. Words cannot express the depth of the guilt and pain I have experienced over the years, even exceeding that of the loss of little Valerie."

Grieving for her precious daughter was hard for Kay. "Being February," Kay says. "I couldn't get out much. The following days were very lonely and bleak for me. My mother-in-law, however, came up with an idea I shall never forget. She brought me a box of old photographs from her family, the Aurand family, and I absolutely loved going through them. It proved to be a very uplifting time of my grief until came the Spring when I could 'breathe.'"

As people do, they tried to comfort Kay. One comment that was made was not helpful, though. Someone said to her, "But you can have another baby."

"Another baby," Kay says, "Never replaced Valerie." Kay had two boys after Valerie passed and adored raising them.

What role did faith play in Kay's grieving process? "I did not know Jesus as Savior at that time in my life, but I knew there was a God and I prayed for another baby."

Kay never attended grief counseling.

Kay has ways today of coping with her daughter's passing. "Even today, I go to her grave," Kay says. I regret not having a picture of her and this is grief that will go with me to my grave. But I know I will see her again. I will always and ever encourage mothers of babies who are dying, to see, hold, and have photos of their baby. Today, this is encouraged."

Grieving for Valerie was different from other grieving Kay faced in her life. It did, however, help her to understand how her natural mother felt when she lost her first baby girl to pneumonia.

Regrets about how Kay dealt with her grieving linger today. "I had no encouragement from the medical community to see my little girl and I did not know the Lord at that time in my life," Kay says. "So I did not understand many things about grief. Another thing we had to deal with was finding a place to bury her. In the end, my mother offered my dad's space. We buried her with my dad."

Kay accepted Christ as her Savior in 1972 and now says she has learned many things from Valerie's passing. More than anything, she learned to share her experiences with others who are going through similar grief.

In 1980, twenty-one years had passed since the birth and death of Kay's baby. "It was September," Kay says. "Nearing our twenty-first wedding anniversary. My husband had an appointment at the hospital to see about the pain he had been having on his left side. He was quickly admitted to the hospital, having been diagnosed with leukemia. After 20 months of treatment and five remissions, my husband went to be with the Lord."

After his death, Kay pondered a discussion she had years ago with a friend about how they would deal with the loss of a child. Her friend said that she could handle losing her husband easier than she could losing a child. Kay had agreed with her friend that losing a child might be much harder since the child would not have experienced life. However, Kay had a different conclusion to that conversation now.

"It is a very hard thing losing a child," Kay says. "But I have to say that when our baby died I had my husband by my side." After her husband died, Kay had no one. "I was alone to face my husband's funeral. Yes, there were two sons with whom we were later blessed. There were family members and friends. And, though I would never downplay the pain of the loss of a child, from my own experience, I have felt that it was much harder to lose my companion, my mate, the father of my kids, and my best friend.

At the end of the day, it is Jesus and my relationship to him that has gotten me through. During the course of my husband's illness, I had placed a poster on our family room wall. It pictured a water skier deluged under a huge wave. It was inscribed with a scripture from Isaiah 43:2. When we trust Jesus and his promises we will find that there is a rainbow at the end of every trial."

Christy Lee Young
Age - 26 Weeks Gestation
8/22/1977 to 8/22/1977

As told by: Carolyn Teal, Christy's mother

Precious Christy, due in November, 1977, was still-born August 22, 1977 because of the RH factor. Prior to her death, the doctors had determined from amniocentesis that Christy needed an intrauterine transfusion. A transfusion attempt was made but the needle went into the placenta instead of the baby, causing the placenta to hemorrhage. An ultrasound confirmed that Christy had died. Carolyn never got to see or hold her baby due to the length of time Christy was deceased before being delivered by cesarean section.

Carolyn's initial response was that she wished that the medical staff could do something to save her baby. "It was really hard for me to accept that there was nothing to be done for her. In the back of my mind I was thinking that maybe they could do something to save Christy. But that was unrealistic.

I was depressed after that because at the time they did the emergency Cesarean Section, they also did a tubal ligation. Here I was, not even 27 years old, and it was the end of my childbearing years. I didn't want to do anything but lie in bed."

Carolyn had at home, a two and a half year old son Dwayne, and a younger son Brian. Little Brian was still like a baby and helped fulfill Carolyn's desperate need for a baby to hold.

"My grieving got to the point where I did it in private. It bothers you forever. I think of what I could have done differently," Carolyn says. "Could I have done something else?"

What made her feel better? "Having her two sons to take care of was a help for her. "They were my reasons for going on and snapping out of it because they needed me. That was a blessing. Had this been my first-born baby that I had lost, I think the depression would have gone on longer."

What made her feel worse? "One time I got an advertisement in the mail from a mortuary and I thought that the hospital had notified them that we had a loss and might need their services. They hadn't. It was just a coincidence but it bothered me and upset me. It was also hard for me to be around my friend who was pregnant at the same time I was. She ended up having a little girl and that was difficult. It was also hard for her to see me having the loss. She didn't know what to say or how to bring it up.

One of the good things for me was that I was very involved with my son, Brian, in an Easter Seals Infant program. So, I had been in contact with other mothers who had experienced a loss. Being able to talk with those moms was really helpful. We could talk freely. I knew their pain and they knew my pain. We could open up to each other. They truly understood."

What did people say or do that didn't help? "There were some that said, 'It was probably a blessing because there were probably going to be problems so it was for the best. How could you have coped with another child who had a problem?' But I didn't look at it that way. Someone else said, 'At least you have two more children. You should enjoy them.' That didn't help. It didn't make the pain go away. You're not going to replace your child. It's not like a vase that you break. You love each one of your children."

What did people do that helped? "The medical community that cried with me helped. I loved them for their compassion and their willingness to let down their reserve and be human with me. That meant a lot. To know that they cared so deeply."

Carolyn's faith played a big role in her grieving. "I strongly believe that there is a heaven," Carolyn says. "I strongly believe that there is a God and there is an afterlife. I feel certain that I am going to meet Christy some day in heaven and that somehow we're going to know each other. I don't know what she will look like but we're going to know each other. I believe that it is a better place and that you are healed."

Carolyn didn't attend any grief counseling and cannot remember any being offered to her.

How does she cope now with Christy's loss? "I try not to think about it too much. I keep it in the back of my mind. Way in the back. I feel like it was a valuable experience that I went through because it allows me to understand and be compassionate towards some-one else who experienced the same loss. I know they will feel that ache forever. That little part of them will always be missing. I'm probably blessed to have had the experience."

Grieving for a child was different for Carolyn from other grief that she experienced. "Christy never had a chance," Carolyn says. "She had her whole life ahead of her. The grief was totally different."

What did Carolyn learn from her grieving experience? She learned that grief must be dealt with when it happens. "After I lost her," Carolyn says, "And people would come to visit in the hospital, they didn't want to talk about it and I didn't talk about it. We put on this facade that there wasn't really anything wrong. I suppressed it. But then at night, I would have nightmares. Once, in the middle of the night, I found myself running down the hallway, I think because I suppressed it so much during the day, trying to pretend that nothing was wrong. I was haunted by nightmares for a long time after that because I wouldn't deal with it. You shouldn't do that. It's not good or healthy. You need to acknowledge your feelings. You learn what grieving really feels like and hopefully you can help someone else who is going through it."

Carolyn has some specific advice for the readers of this book. "Don't be afraid to grieve. Grieve freely. Don't put pressure on yourself as to where you think you should be in the grieving process. It's not a steady thing. You'll bounce back from one point to another. It's not a smooth progression. Everybody grieves in a different way. Don't let others tell you how to grieve. Whatever you feel is right for you. Just don't let others tell you what you should be doing or how you should be feeling. Only you know that. Validate your own feelings and beliefs. Go with it. You know what is best for you. I don't think anyone else has the right to tell someone who is grieving how they should feel."

Baby Boy Zerick
Age - 2 ½ months gestation
2/16/1948 to 2/16/1948

~

Timothy Dale Zerick
Age - 8 months gestation
1/5/1961 to 1/5/1961

~

Lisa Garrod
Age - 41
2/1/1963 to 6/5/2005

As told by: Lura Zerick, the mother of Baby Boy,
Timothy, and Lisa.

Lura Zerick knows something about parental griev-ing. She suffered two stillbirths (1948 and 1961) and in 2005, her grown daughter Lisa died after suffering a seizure. Lura continues to trust God for her daily walk, claiming that is what keeps her going.

Lisa's seizure disorder started spontaneously when her first child was two years old. She had stopped taking her seizure medication prior to the fatal convul-sion because she didn't like the way it made her feel. Therefore, without medication, she suffered seizures intermittently. The day she died, Lisa's husband had found his wife dead on the kitchen floor from a seizure when he came home for lunch. Lura was at home when she received the phone call from another daughter that Lisa had passed.

Lura was understandably shocked. "I could hardly believe it," she says. "But then again, I've had other grieving, so I knew it was true. The Bible tells us to have a prayerful attitude and that is my greatest comfort. To stay in a prayerful attitude. Whatever I feel in my heart, I can pour out to God. It still hurts, but at the same time, I trust God."

What was Lura doing that made her feel better? "Only prayer," she says. "That helps me no matter what is happening. I've learned that there are some things I have no control over, but I know who does. You try to forget the negative things and remember the good things."

What made her feel worse? "I feel worse because that morning that Lisa passed, I had thought about calling her and I didn't because I knew how busy she was. I regretted not calling her because even if she had been real busy I could have spoken to her."

There were things that people said that made her feel worse. "Someone said, 'She's better off.' That might be true but that didn't help. They mean well but they don't know what to say unless they have experienced it."

What helped? "When people gave me a hug and didn't speak," Lura says. "Because that showed me a better understanding than words can. I can't think of anything they said because I'm not sure if there are any words that help. People in general don't know what to say because it's not their pain."

Lura's faith played a big role in her grieving. "It's the most important thing in my life. That's the only comfort there is as far as I'm concerned. Any pain that I have I can share it with God. That helps with whatever's wrong. I had a lot of lessons to learn because I walked away from God after my first son was stillborn. Out of my youthful ignorance of spiritual things, I blamed God. We're so eager to blame somebody for everything. I didn't go to church for about ten years. I was mad at God. I was the youngest of eight and always wanted a big family. I wanted to be a super wife and mom. By the time my second miscarriage came along, I had grown spiritually and was much better able to accept it than I did the first one. It bothered me. I was disappointed and hurt, but not as bad as the first one. All these negative things just pushed me closer to God."

Lura went to a counselor after the second stillbirth of a baby she named Timothy. "It was for my grief and also the problems I had in my marriage," Lura says. "It was a Christian psychologist and it helped. I had spent years in depression from the stillbirths and a bad marriage I was in. But I have the peace of God now. It feels good to laugh."

Lura tells how, in the depressive state she had been in, she tried suicide twice by taking pills and had her stomach pumped, which saved her life. "I was in a deep well of depression and couldn't get out. Now I have joy in my life," Lura says. "I know whose I am."

Today, Lura copes with her daughter's passing by being thankful for the years they had together. "I know she had accepted Jesus and I will see her again," Lura says. "Any negative thing I have happen, I talk to the Lord about it. He knows what to do. When I don't know what to do, I give it to the Lord."

Grieving for her children was different for Lura from other grieving she had experienced. "They were my heart," Lura says. "My children were part of my dreams and my hopes for a loving family."

Lura regrets that she turned away from the Lord after her first miscarriage. "I threw those years away and they could have been productive," Lura says. "The only thing is that I can now help others who are grieving."

What would Lura say to readers of this story? "Don't be so bullheaded that you won't listen to anyone else. Trust the Lord. It sounds like I'm saying something that is just words, but in truth that is everything. Sometimes you can't understand why things happen and I think there are things we can't understand why. We just have to learn through spiritual growth."

"I used to call her, 'Lisa, my laughing girl,' because she laughed a lot," Lura says.

Jared Jim Hodgins
Age - 16
7/23/1981 to 4/29/1998

As told by: Jim and Lisa Hodgins,
Jared's father and stepmother.

In many ways, Jared was a typical teenager. He loved spending time with his friends riding around town and playing music. After school, on April 29, 1998, he went with his friends to play golf. Since there was not enough room in the front of the truck for all of them, Jared sat in the back of the truck with the golf clubs. While riding through an intersection, the truck hit a curb, and Jared was thrown out of the back of the truck into the path of an oncoming Mustang car. He was killed instantly.

Jim and Lisa were at a coffee shop when they received the news. Jim stepped outside to take the call and learned that his son was killed.

"Initially I went numb," Jim says. "I asked how it happened and then broke down crying."

Lisa remembers that when her husband came back into the restaurant, he told her what had happened. "I remember that he just froze. I told him to wait in the car while I closed the bill. We then left to go be with Jared's younger brothers. A few weeks later, we learned he had accepted the Lord. We found great peace in that."

A week after he heard the bad news, Jim had to go accept a bowling trophy for Jared and say a few words in his name. The driver of the truck carrying Jared the night he was killed was present there, and Jim let him know that he had forgiven him.

"Part of the grief is our own selfishness," Jim says. "If you look at where Jared is now versus being here, you must ask, where would you rather be? We're not here to adjust, judge, or reconstruct God's plan. His plan is his plan. And if that was his plan, who am I to say? There are other things you can focus on."

"About a month after Jared passed," Lisa says, "We brought the boys to a children's grief counselor. Jim sat in on the sessions. They only went a few times and felt it didn't help them. I think it was too soon. They were still in shock and numb. We did our best to try and help the younger boys who were 12 and 13 at the time. Lots of hugs and tears. We tried to keep the atmosphere positive and they were encouraged to share their fears with us. Initially, I think everyone was so shook up that driving in cars was a little scary. A sudden death is like that. It always makes you face your own mortality."

"The journey never ends," Jim says. "God says he will never give you anything that you can't handle. I believe there will be a gain somewhere. The grieving process was wavy for us. You have your good days and you have your bad days. It doesn't take much to trigger a thought. I can have times where I can laugh and joke around, and other times I sit out back and cry my eyes out. Men, we sometimes have a problem processing it. We bury it. It's like a dog with a bone. We bury it. It doesn't stay buried, it comes up. It's better to face it and go through the pain."

"My observation with Jim," Lisa says. "Is that he was always joking around and humming, fooling around and laughing. He went a whole year where he said, 'I don't think I could ever joke again.' He didn't have that joy but, over time, it's come back. We focused our energy on getting a law changed to make it illegal to ride in the back of a pickup truck. I contacted different congressmen and we were trying to get it changed and a bill was drafted but twice it would get stuck. It's still on the back burner for us but we are going to address it again."

"That's the thing. You have all this energy and what are you going to do with it? You can either do something good with it or not. I think times like this bring you closer to the Lord," Jim said.

There were things that Lisa and Jim did that made them feel better. "We talked about it," Jim says.

"And we put Jared's picture on the shelf next to the door," Lisa says. "We saw it every time we went out and when we came back in."

"It was there for a long time for everybody's sake," Jim adds.

"And I made a scrapbook about Jared," Lisa says. "It took five years because it was so hard to do. At Jared's funeral, there were doves, and every now and again I see two doves together in the back yard. It happens at odd times and when something will happen with the children, I look up and see the two doves, I think, well, Jared's seeing what's going on with the other children. I don't believe in reincarnation but it reminds me of Jared and his cousin because they died a year apart from each other."

Both Lisa and Jim found prayer to be helpful for them.

Things that made them feel worse? "I drank," Jim said. "That made me feel worse. My emotions got skewed. I was more apt to let my emotions out. It's okay to grieve. It's okay to feel bad. I still miss him and wonder what he'd be like now."

There were things that people said and did that helped the couple. "The emotions and the hugs. The look in the eye. The quiet communication," Jim says. "That's what really helped. Someone said to us, 'He's in a better place,' " Jim says. "That helped, too. And once, in our Grief Share group, I told a woman that it was the eighth anniversary of Jared's passing. The woman said, 'Why don't you look at it like this. This is the eighth anniversary of his being with the Lord. How's that?' That helped remind me, my glass can be half full not half empty."

Did Lisa and Jim attend any grief counseling? As of this writing they are attending a 13-week course called Grief Share. "It's an excellent course," Jim says. "It increases your love for human beings."

What role did faith play in the Hodgins' grief? "For me, it was monumental," Lisa says. "Sometimes, there's no words and I don't even have words to pray. I'm just crying to God but I know he understands."

"I wouldn't trade one tear for a million laughs," Jim says. "Because that one tear can become but a flood of Holy water on your face. I sometimes ask myself, 'What would Jared say if he could talk to me?' I think the answer is very simple. He'd say, 'If you knew where I was at right now, and if you knew what was here, you wouldn't want me to come back at all.'"

"He'd say, 'I'm having a great time,'" Lisa adds.

Coping today for Jim and Lisa is a process of transferring the emotions into a positive outlay of actions. "I can sympathize with others because I have more feelings and love for others emotionally," Jim says. "I seem to understand people a little bit better. I don't wish he was back here because of where he is. There's nothing pressing me down now."

Looking through the scrapbook about Jared that Lisa put together for Jim, the couple basks in the photos and joy they find in the memories they have of him.

"I'm glad I have my wife," Jim says. "Having her has been a great blessing from God. We complement each other."

Grieving for Jared was different from other grieving they experienced. "I think it was different because of the bond," Lisa says.

"Because it's what you put into them," Jim says. "The quality time that you spend with them and the exchange of emotions that you have invested in them. I think that is what makes the difference in your grief."

"I remember feeling," Lisa says, "That because Jared wasn't my own child, that people didn't appreciate my loss that I felt. Some people just didn't think I could relate. My husband did, but others didn't. His loss, because he went before his parents, was out of life's norm." Lisa felt that her grief as a step-parent wasn't validated by some others.

Lisa and Jim learned many things from the grieving experience. Lisa says she learned how to show more empathy for others in general. "I learned not to let the small stuff bother me so much because they could be gone," She says. "We value our relationships with people more and the time we spend with them. Make that time count while you have it." Jim agrees. "And we came through it," Lisa says. "It took time. We had to get through the milestones."

"I learned," Jim says, "How much is out of your control. After Jared passed, I learned that life is not about me. I look outward now. It's about them. The transfer of feelings so people can relate."

What would Lisa and Jim like the readers of this book to know? "It just seems so dark and overwhelming with pain at first, so raw, and an open wound," Lisa says. "You will get through it. You don't see it right now because you are walking through that darkness, but there is a light. You just keep hanging in there. God was our light through that darkness. You take it moment to moment, day to day. Everything is a little milestone but you will get through. Just keep walking forward."

Jim says, "Just keep it on the surface. Take small steps. A journey doesn't start until you make the first step and healing doesn't start until you take the first small steps. I wouldn't take too big a steps. It's okay to cry. It's okay to be angry for a period of time. Don't beat yourself up."

"That's one of the biggest things I see," Lisa says. "Grieving parents say, 'Oh I cry too much.' You don't want to stay that way long term but there are times when you want to just crawl under the covers and cry all day. Just don't have such high expectations for yourself. You should keep busy and find something to do that helps expend some of that energy into a positive outlook."

"Try to avoid self-pity," Jim says. "It's tough to face but you feel sorry for yourself because that loved one's not there. It's easy to say now, but it would have been tough for me to say when Jared died. Realize what you do have left."

Jared is greatly missed.

Robert E. Best
Age - 53
9/21/1953 to 9/4/2007

As told by: Willard and Rodell Best, mother and father.

Robert was the first black Lieutenant on the Melbourne Fire Department and was well respected by those with whom he worked. Besides his parents, two brothers, a sister, and other family members, he had three children, three stepchildren, and a wife who were left behind when he passed away from lung cancer.

Robert suffered from a cough for a long time before he finally went to the doctor to find out what was causing it. It was most noticeable the last month of his life. "My husband would go fishing with Robert and during the last month, he would come home and say, 'Willard, Robert coughed so badly he had to rest before he got back to the truck.'" Both parents were worried about their son's condition.

Prior to that Thursday, Robert had gone for an X-ray. He got the call that they found something on the X-ray and he went back for a CAT Scan the next day.

Robert pulled the X-rays from his truck to show his parents what the doctors had found. "This is what he showed me," Robert had said. His parents were shocked when they saw the results. Willard had thought that Robert would live through it because her brother had lung cancer, too, and had survived.

The Sunday after learning about the lung cancer, Robert was admitted to the hospital and placed on oxygen. On Monday, Willard and her daughter slept overnight in his room in the hospital Intensive Care Unit to be with him. Robert passed away about 10 a.m. on Tuesday.

"My first response to his death was denial. It couldn't be. No way. Not Robert. Disbelief," Willard says. "It was hard to believe it. Then I'd be crying because I was angry with him. Maybe he knew he had cancer but I don't know whether he knew it or not. At first, I was in this denial. Then it got to me and I got angry with him. And sometimes now, it's hard to believe. Parents always look for their children to bury them. Not the other way."

Rodell had a similar response. "Well, at first it was bad. It was rough on me. But, after awhile, I realized that by him dying, it's something we all have to do. I really grieve, though, because me and him were really close. We did a lot of things together. Anything that he wanted to do that was really important, he would always come to me and ask me, 'Dad, what should I do. Should I do it this way?' I would tell him what I thought. But him and me were so close. We did everything together. We went fishing together and just about every place he went, when he wasn't working, he'd come by for me to go with him. It was rough on me but I realized that bad things happen. Although, you know, he had to go through it. There comes a time when you have to just go on with your life. You won't forget about it, but you have to go on with your life. A day doesn't pass that I don't think about him. Every night before I go to bed and I'm praying, I always think about Robert. Every night and every morning when I get up, I think about it. To me you can only grieve for so long and then you have to go on with your life."

What did Willard and Rodell do that made them feel better? "I still cry a lot," Rodell says. "Just thinking about the good times we had together and how caring he was, helps. Robert was a caring person. Not only for his family but also the community."

Faith played such a big part in their grieving process. "If I didn't have Christ in my life," Willard says, "I couldn't make it. I couldn't make it. He knows the hurt and he knows what you're going through. You must trust him." Rodell agreed with his wife.

What did people say that helped? Willard had some examples. "One neighbor said, 'I've been praying for you.' Another person said, 'You're gonna see him again.' And my daughter always says, 'You're gonna see him again and you must focus on the memories that you have.' And we do. Anything that was going on, he was always there. A friend spoke well of Robert and told me I should be proud of him because he was such a good son. That helped a lot."

Rodell says, "People always had an encouraging word such as, 'The Lord will see you through this.' Another person said, 'Me and my family are going to be praying for you and your family. We're gonna pray that you make it through this and with prayer, you will make it through.' Encouraging words from people help us."

"The things that made me feel better are, I know that, although he passed away, I know that we'll be together again, and I'll see him again," Rodell says. "I also think about the things that Robert did for me when he was alive and I know he'd still be doing those things for me. Sometimes I get all confused and I go off by myself in the backyard because, really, I didn't know what to do."

"There's no right and wrong way to grieve," Willard says. "Sometimes you just got to cry. You just got to let it out. One Sunday I was in church and the tears were just rolling down. I cried through the whole service. A lady came up and prayed for me and said, 'You're gonna be alright. Just let it all out.' Sometimes, though, when I think that he's gone, it's like it's just new to you again."

What did Robert's parents do that made them feel worse? "I try not to think about the day he passed," Willard says. "That just brings all the memories back so I just try to blot it out of my mind. I try not to think about it, but sometimes it just comes back and I have to push it away."

Rodell says, "I would avoid going by his house where he lived because I knew if I went by there, I would break down. I avoided going by his house for a long time. If I had to go out, I would take another route so I wouldn't be going by his house."

"I had a picture of Robert out but he (Rodell) took it down. I just wanted to look at it but it was just too hard for him," Willard says.

How was grieving for Robert different from other types of grief Willard and Rodell experienced? "When my mom died," Willard says, "It bothered me but nothing bothered me like this. I haven't felt such hurt. I don't know how to explain it. It's so different. It's a hurt that goes deeper than deep. And the way it happened so fast, I didn't have time to ask questions. It just happened so fast to even realize. But I thank God it happened the way it did and that he didn't linger, suffering."

Robert's parents couldn't remember anything that people said that did not help.

How do Willard and Rodell cope now? "When I think about the things that we'd done together and the way he did it. We've had good times and I think about what a good fellow he was. That's how I'm learning to cope," Willard says. "You know, just think about the good things and the memories. Me and my daughter talk about him all the time. I just think about how good he was. I dwell on the good things."

"I can cope with it pretty good now, knowing he wouldn't want us to grieve," Rodell says. "He'd want us to go on with our lives. I think about the way that he would want us to feel and carry on with our lives. I can cope with it better now than when it happened."

Do they have any regrets about how they grieved? Is there anything they would change? "If I could change anything, it would be to bring him back," Willard says.

What did Rodell and Willard learn from this experience? "To ask questions," Willard says. "I'd ask more questions of Robert. I didn't ask what the doctors told Robert and now I wonder about that. I'd talk about it more. I think he wanted to keep it from us because he wouldn't want us to worry."

Rodell learned to pay more attention to the kids that he has left. "I ask them more questions now. Whether they tell you or not, I learned to ask more questions.

To see if anything is wrong. I never did ask Robert a lot of questions. I'd tell him to get checked for his bad cough but I didn't ask him a lot of questions about it. Maybe he wouldn't have told me anyway. I would feel better if I would have asked him more questions than I did. But I used to tell him a lot about how I appreciated everything he did for me and his mother."

Both Willard and Rodell had something they would want readers to know. "You can never be prepared for this. I would tell parents that if they have to cry, then cry," Willard says. "I would tell them that if they don't know God, then you need to get to know him because he is the only one who can get you through this. Believe that your child is in a better place. You'll get to see him one day. Some days I could holler and scream but I know it wouldn't do any good. So think about the memories. You don't get used to it but you adjust your life to it. You take it one day at a time."

"The only thing I can think of right now is that I am glad my son's name is in this book because one day you might have to go through the same thing and I'm glad you're reading this book and you'll know how to cope with it," Rodell says.

Dennis Richard McMahon III (Captain)
Age - 27
9/4/1954 to 7/10/1982

~

Michael "Mike" Jerome McMahon (Lt. Colonel)
Age - 41
10/22/1963 to 11/27/2004

*As told by: Dennis, "Mac" McMahon, their father
(Retired Lt. Colonel - 37 years 8 months and 22 days).*

Mac McMahon's sons, Dennis and Mike, were United States Military Academy alumni and served proudly in their country's service. Dennis was a 1976 West Point graduate and Mike graduated from the academy in 1985. Their passing came 22 years apart but their father, Mac, recalls each one very well.

Dennis played on a military rugby team, traveling with his teammates to other military bases for matches. On July 10, 1982, after the match was over, Dennis and his fiancee joined others at the host team club to celebrate the game. Dennis could not drive, having had too much to drink, so he was in the passenger seat of his pickup truck, slouched over. His fiancee was driving them home and lost control of the vehicle, which went off the road. Dennis was thrown out after the truck rolled the second time of six rollovers, and was crushed beneath it.

Mac, a retired military man (WW II, Korea, and Vietnam veteran) was in Seattle at a marriage encounter convention, when he heard about the accident. At first he was upset because, "I thought maybe his fiancee was drunk driving," Mac says. "The more details I received about the game and Dennis being unable to drive, I had to accept the fact that he was intelligent enough to know he couldn't drive.

"Dennis's fiancee was hospitalized so I went to see her in Georgia after my son's burial. While her mother sat at the foot of the bed and cried, she told me the whole story. I knew the girl felt guilty. For myself, I had to relieve my anger or animosity of blaming her. I started to feel pain for her. Her grandfather had a heart attack after learning about the accident and was in the same hospital. Dennis's fiancee and I went down to see him at her request, because her grandfather loved Dennis as if he was his own grandson. At this time I was in active ministry at my church and the fiancee asked me to bless her grandfather. It was a very emotional thing. Pain-relieving. It took a lot of my pain away. Yes, I was angry that it all happened. I had been blaming her, but it was a larger relief to me to understand and accept the one I had been blaming. That was the beginning of healing for me. That helped me back then and it helps me now."

As time went on, Dennis's mother was unable to cope with her son's death and Mac found the most difficult time for him was in trying to ease his wife's pain. "I got more upset because his mother never got over it," Mac says. "She sat and grieved the loss and held onto it for so long. In less than six months, she was diagnosed with cancer and died a few years after that. Her grief harmed her health."

The response of friends and family made Mac feel

better. "My good friend brought Dennis's body back home from Georgia to us. The number of family and friends who came from all over, and the closeness of our community, made this more tolerable. I believe this also made it easier for me. Ministering, being open and accepting, helps you get through your own grief and then receive back from others."

What made Mac feel worse? "I kept working," Mac says. "It was part of my guilt feelings. When my wife died, I gave my business away. I retired and went into a depression. Nothing was important to me anymore. After awhile, I started trying to live again."

Mac's faith played a large role in his grieving process. "You bring the ministry into what gets you through the grieving," he says. "Friends eventually introduced me to another woman and I married her. Praise the Lord that there are those who care enough to try to help you get through it."

Mac did not attend grief counseling but did have some talks with his priest, which helped. But, 22 years later, after losing two wives to cancer, Mac faced the loss of a second child.

Mike, another of Mac's sons, the recipient of a Purple Heart and other military medals, was the most senior officer killed in Afghanistan. He was a Cavalry Aviator and took his squadron from the Hawaiian Islands to Afghanistan. On November 27, 2004, after a meeting at Headquarters Bagrham, he boarded a government supply aircraft, piloted by a government-contracted pilot, which crashed at 14,600 feet, into an Afghanistan mountain. Mac was at home when an Army major came to tell him the news of Mike's death.

Mac remembers his son's love of the work he was doing with the local Afghanistan population and how many friends he made amongst the people. "Mike was often invited to their homes and meetings and sometimes entertained them by juggling oranges."

Mac's initial response? "I blamed the government for his death."

The state of Connecticut lowered the flag half-mast for a week in honor of Mike and the West Hartford community has a memorial walk stone dedicated to him. While these are honors for his son, Mac finds them to be, "Painful in a way. I found that, the amount of time you want to refuse or reject or not accept reminders of his death is partially controlled by your reaching out and accepting others."

Coping now for Mac is summed up in one sentence —"God takes care of me."

Grieving for a child was different for him from other kinds of grieving he experienced. "We look to blame someone and if we don't find forgiveness through one method or another, we won't get over it."

"God is still taking care of me," he says. "I still have my faith, my friends, and my community. I keep thanking God. We have still received blessings from Him and still have the time and ability to help others understand why God has us here and not those who have died. My faith has kept me going. I'm a lucky guy and have a wonderful life."

What has he learned from his losses? "You have to accept responsibility for your decisions, also," Mac says. "Yes, I could have said to Mike, 'I'm not going to let you go into combat,' but my love for him enabled me to let him do what he wanted to do."

Mac has things that he would like the reader to know. "Basically, examine your own grief and own propensity to blame others. Be fair. Be faithful. Communicate through your faith and take responsibility for decisions that you have made. If you examine and accept rather than continuing to blame, you will be blessed."

William "Billy" Robert Bonwell
Age - 25
9/15/1980 to 5/20/2006

As told by: Cheryl Bonwell, Billy's mother.

On a clear, sunny Saturday afternoon, Billy was driving home from work as he had done so often before. His pickup truck crossed the center of the line and hit a Jersey barrier head on. He died at the accident scene at 4:20 p.m. The cause of death was attributed to blunt force head trauma.

Cheryl and her husband Bill were watching television about 8:30 p.m. when the police knocked at their door with the bad news. They handed Bill a small slip of paper with a state police phone number on it and said that there had been a horrific accident and to call that number. "When we heard the news," Cheryl says, "we screamed and screamed in disbelief."

Their church family, upon hearing what happened,

immediately came that night. Three church ministers visited the Bonwell home to offer support and guidance. "They offered us whatever help we would need," Cheryl says. "We were and are blessed to have such awesome support from family and friends."

The head of the church pastors had a son die about a year before Billy so he understood what Bill and Cheryl would be going through and counseled them about what he knew.

What helps the family now? "There is a place that we seem to find some peace," Cheryl says. "It is at a campground where we have a trailer. It is our sanctuary and get-away. And treasuring the memories of Billy is something no one can take away. It also helps that Billy's grave is decorated. I make wreaths and other things and put them on the grave." Billy's grave is always decorated.

Cheryl feels bad when people would not want to listen to her talk about memories that she has of Billy. "It is just a way of keeping his memory alive," she says. "I look back at all the struggles of Billy's life and how he had overcome them and tried to go forward. He never got to do the many things he set out to do. He was on the right path when he died."

What did people say or do that helped? "We have several friends at church who have lost children and are there for us and know what to do and say at the bad times," Cheryl says.

What didn't help? "Someone said, 'You were only his parents,'" Cheryl says. "Others said, 'You have other children,' and 'He did get to do some things in his life,' and some have said, 'When are you going to get over it and quit talking about him?'"

Cheryl says, "My answer is, 'Never!'"

Faith played a very important role in the lives of Bill, Cheryl, and Billy's younger brother and sister. "We would be nowhere without it," Cheryl says. "We have never questioned why God took him as it is not our right to. He completed his time on earth and God needed him in heaven. I believe that he (Billy) is watching over us and enjoying riding his Harley motorcycle across the sky."

Both of the parents attended grief counseling provided by their minister. They went as a couple and, at times, separately. "We both felt he was very highly qualified because he lost a child, too," Cheryl says. "He was and is a great help to us. Many who have lost children offered to go with us to a support group. We have not done that yet. We have friends we can talk to who understand."

How do they cope now with their child's passing? "Every day is a challenge in itself. Some are more difficult than others," Cheryl says. "I can't say that it gets easier. We try to stay busy as it consumes time in a positive way. We try to go forward one step at a time. Bill and I do some church activities and some campground activities to help out and Bill is the Boy Scout leader for our younger son's troop. We try to do things that are good and positive." Bill is also helping his son Brandon in working towards his Eagle Award of the Boy Scouts of America.

Was grieving for a child different for the couple from grieving for others? The family suffered the death of Cheryl's father just 27 days before Billy died. "I can't honestly answer this because of that," Cheryl says. "I knew that dad was dying from prostate cancer and I got to spend time going places with him and talking with him for nine months before he died," Cheryl says. "Billy died very unexpectedly. I carried Billy for nine months and, as a parent, was to protect and nurture him. I was not able to do this for him. But I never really got to grieve my dad because of Billy's death."

Both Cheryl and Bill have some regrets about the way that they grieved. "We have regretted that we were not more assertive in some of the details concerning Billy's funeral."

Was there anything that Cheryl and Bill learned from the loss of their son? "Yes. We try to listen to others, not ask a lot of questions or judge others," Cheryl and Bill say. "The key here is that someone else always has a worse situation than you. There is a reason for all things and we have no right to question 'why' or 'what is the purpose?' There is a purpose and God knows what it is. We try to reach out to others in difficult experiences to help, if possible, or just be there to listen, which is a very important thing."

Cheryl and Bill would like the readers to know some specific things. "The loss of a child, no matter what age or circumstances, is truly 'Hell on earth,'" Cheryl says. "It is a never-ending pain of the heart and nothing is ever the same. Some days are better and some are worse than others. It is part of God's plan that the loss of a child happened to us. We have no right to question why. Some day we will be reunited with our loved ones when God chooses. It is our faith that guides us. We are blessed to have the love and support of those who truly care about us to uplift us in our time of need. The hurt and pain remain with you each and every day, for nothing that you do is the same."

Andy Tant
Age - 16
8/8/1980 to 12/8/1996

As told by: Dianne and Mike Tant, Andy's parents.

While en route to church on a Sunday morning, Andy, the youngest in a family of four children, fell asleep at the wheel and hit another car head on. According to the attending physicians, 16-year-old Andy's condition was, "Almost beyond hope." Attempts were made to stabilize his vital signs but tests indicated that there was no brain activity.

"Our world changed on December 8, 1996," Andy's parents report. "In a brief period of a few hours our entire perspective on life was altered. The universe as we knew it was no longer the same." Dianne and Mike tell how a parent's worst nightmare happened to them and they could not imagine their ability to handle that kind of tragedy.

"We learned that Andy had been transported by helicopter to the hospital. As we traveled to the hospital, not knowing his condition, we prayed over and over for God to spare his life. The anxiety was unbearable and those 30 minutes or so in transit were some of the worst of our lives."

Andy's parents describe the pain that they felt was, "Awful. Real, physical pain." When their son passed away, the sense of loss they felt weighed heavily upon them. They asked themselves, "What about those prayers we said while driving? Wasn't God listening?" Both report that in the midst of the crushing news, they felt a real peace. The peace that passes understanding, which had always been theory to them, became a reality in their existence. "It is a peace that the world may not understand," they report. "However, it is just as real as the paper you now have in your hand. God did not fail to hear our prayers. He showed us that His plan was different and more glorious than our desires. And, He gave us the grace and faith to accept His will."

According to the Tants, Andy's death brought their focus forth onto heaven. "We long to be there with him," they report. When people ask them how they know he is in heaven, they tell them that although man is plagued with doubts, God has given them the gift of faith and that faith is, "the substance of things hoped for, the evidence of things not seen."

Dianne and Mike believe that, as Christians, their call is to "Endure. God sanctifies our endurance for fruitfulness in the lives of others," they believe. "God is pleased at times to break us into little bits so that each bit, in turn, may become food from which others may draw nourishment and flourish. None of us is exempt."

The Tants believe that pain shapes us into Christ's

image. "All of this is counter to modern Christianity that expects no suffering," they say. "Such a philosophy makes human happiness the highest object. This view loses sight of the role of pain in sanctification. God trains his children to share in his holiness through pain and suffering."

Andy's parents are not saying, "It is not really so bad. Because it is. Some people say nothing because they find the topic too painful for themselves," the Tants say. "They fear it will break them down." However, Andy's parents are comforted in their grief when people come close to them and cry with them.

Memories of their son's life and the funny things about him comfort them—even times of terrible disobedience and mischief. "I love it when people tell me 'stories' about Andy because they knew him," Dianne says. "After Andy died, the gift of life became far more precious. Our relationships with our children and each other as husband and wife have become even more valuable. It's amazing how death brings what is most important to the forefront of our lives." The Tants want to go back in time and they want Andy back with them. They believe, however, that unlike unbelievers, their road is not back in time.

The faith that Mike and Dianne held was critical to their daily lives. "The significance of our faith," Dianne says. "Is a long-term relationship with Jesus and the gospel which has taught and informed our faith over the years in preparation for tragedy and disappointment. There was no 'great revelation of knowledge' that God gave us at the moment, just the faithfulness of Him in our lives up to that point. Mike and I have found God to be our source of comfort every day. He has not taken away our pain but He has been with us each step of the way."

Did Dianne and Mike attend any grief counseling? "We just counseled with our Pastors and Christian friends," Dianne says. "I eventually attended a Mom's Support Group and was the President for a couple of years. This helped me to see the hopelessness of those parents who do not know the Lord and have no confidence in anything beyond themselves. They had very little comfort. As Mike and I had much comfort, we comforted others."

What would the Tants want the readers to think about?

1. Make time for your family. They are a priority.

2. Make time to be alone with your surviving children.

3. Encourage your children, (especially younger) to talk. Try to understand their feelings.

4. Continue to grow spiritually. Reflect upon God's faithfulness and His promises.

5. Pray for your family and with your family. Look to God for strength.

6. Remember that each family member and each day is a gift. Be thankful.

7. Let each member of your family know that you love them. Today.

W. Brandon Seidel
Age - 39
11/24/1968 to 6/20/2008

As told by: Holly Fox Vellekoop, Brandon's mother.

The desperate, lonely feelings that I had while my son was ill caused a measure of fear in my heart. I asked myself, 'If I feel this bad now, how bad is it going to get if he passes away?' When my mother passed away, I was devastated and failed to get a grip on the whole picture for a long time. Understanding the magnitude of that loss, I recognized the potential for even greater sorrow at my son's passing. The nebulous measurements of what my feelings would be eluded me. Before he passed, when I thought of him dying and gone, the horror was such that I pushed it from my mind to free myself up for what needed to be done in daily living. At those times, a dread would weigh my spirit. The jolt to my senses was palpable and yet, I knew that when the time came, it would be worse. How much worse, I did not want to know.

God knew what I was thinking and I reminded Him that I was ready to go should He decide to trade my life for Brandon's life. Bargaining to give up my life and have God leave Brandon here with his family did not work. Not that I thought it would, but I was thinking it so I said it.

One of the things that Brandon and I discussed throughout his two-year battle with cancer was that I would gladly be with him when he needed me to help. If a healing for him from God was not to be, I promised to be there when the end was near. I told him that so often that he finally said, "I know, Mom. You already told me." I wanted him to know that he would have extra help when he needed it most. And, I wanted to do that because of my love for him and his young family.

There were times that God revealed himself to Brandon in mystical ways. One of those happened when Brandon was an inpatient in the hospital, resting in his bed. Brandon told me that he had a feeling like a lightning bolt go through him and the peace of God descended upon him and that it caused him to feel at peace. He claimed that he felt that peace from then on.

Another time was when one of Brandon's doctors entered the hospital room with three colleagues to discuss Brandon's case with him. I looked at them and prayed that God would be with us—that his Holy Spirit would move about the room and speak through them. No sooner had I finished my prayer, the physician began to ask Brandon about his Bible which was on the tray table. Brandon, his physician and I had an open discussion about the Scriptures, St. Paul, and how Paul suffered from the descriptive "thorn in the side," which God never healed. The physician told Brandon that was how it is sometimes. He said that God does not always heal us but He gives us the grace to get through it. He asked Brandon if he understood what he was saying and Brandon said that he did. After the physician and his colleagues left the room, I told Brandon that I believed that was a "God moment." He agreed. It was as if God was speaking through this physician to remind us that

Brandon was not going to be healed but that his grace would be sufficient for what was to happen. Inside, my heart was breaking.

Toward the end, while sitting by Brandon's bed, feeling very much alone, I wondered where God was. I would ask God, 'Where are you? Why don't I feel your presence now?' I was baffled by this. Soon it passed and I was comforted by Him.

We had prayed hard and so had others. Friends, neighbors, friends of friends, relatives and their friends and families, too, sent Brandon's name upward for healing. I shared with Brandon my own visions of heaven and how he would be in communion with family members who had gone before. "Wait for me," I told him. "And be sure and join the greeting party for me when my time comes."

I spent four nights in a row at his bedside, sleeping on the floor, getting about two hours sleep per night, awake, in case he needed something. My son Brian, Brandon's older brother, kept vigil with me. The night before he passed, I went up to my travel trailer behind his home for some rest. I received a call in the morning that Brandon had passed. Brian and I dressed swiftly and went down to his bedside where we witnessed that he had passed away. I touched Brandon's hands, checked his pulse and respirations to be sure, and then touched his still-warm abdomen. He had only just left us.

When others came to comfort his family, I felt myself falling into a cold well of sadness that was deep and dark. Retreating to my trailer to avoid people, I could not entertain the thought of not hearing his voice or seeing him smiling or joking as he once did. I sat and cried and grieved openly and deeply. From my trailer windows, I could see the people who visited his family to pay their respects, many bringing food. Joining others and greeting people and acting as if life would go on was out of the question for me. Many of Brandon's childhood friends came but I was too heartsick to see them. Though I thought life may someday right itself, I just couldn't participate in it at the time.

I told my husband to tell everyone I knew and loved not to call or come see me. I didn't want to see anyone or hear from them. Solitude worked for me.

My heart was broken and it still is. Although I was sure that God's presence was with me, I felt very much alone and shocky. My hands shook at times and nothing outside of Brandon's loss was of importance. I wondered how others could visit, share meals and chatter with people who had come, and some wondered why I could not. I did not want to see or talk to anyone, let alone entertain them with food and beverages. My son was gone and my hostess cup was empty.

There were those who offered advice or a word, some of which helped and some did not. I remember someone asking me if I had any other children. When I said that I had another son, that person said, "That's good." What was implied is that my loss of Brandon was not so serious since I still had another son. How could I tell them that one child does not replace another and that Brandon's place could never be filled?

Another person said to me, "You will see him again in heaven." For me, that was a help because I believe it to be true. Those who said they were praying for me helped, too.

Through hugs and tears, some friends and family confessed their own brand of misery at their experience of the loss of a child. "I understand what you are going through because I lost my child," they said. And, I believed them because of the conviction in their voices. Through their loss, they shared mine.

As they began to put into words the heart-wrenching tale of their own child's passing, each story different from the other, some commonalities appeared. The first such thread was the depth of sadness they were plunged into despite the foreknowledge some experienced. Those whose child died unexpectedly had no less a tale of grief. The circumstances were different, but there was shared terrain that we all walked.

Now, I face each day with his loss. I take it one day at a time, sometimes crying, sometimes not. I feel as though I will never be the same. My life has totally changed and will never be the same either. Never. I get through each twenty-four hours by remembering the boundless love that God has for all of us, thankful for those who have reached out in love to me and my family. I accept and feel God's love and look forward to seeing Brandon again on the other side of heaven's gates.

Junny Rios-Martinez
Age - 11
5/6/1979 to 4/18/1991

As told by: Vicki Rios-Martinez, Junny's mother.

Junny Rios-Martinez's dream was to be a professional surfer on the same level as his surfing hero, Kelly Slater. On April 18, 1991, that dream was extinguished at the hands of convicted child-molester and murderer, Mark Dean Schwab—a case that garnered national attention.

Junny was a charismatic young man who was a magnet for people, drawing them to him wherever he went. "He knew what path he was going to take when he got here and he knew what was going to happen. And he knew he had to touch as many lives as possible, and he did," Vicki says.

Junny's leaving this world at the hands of a killer started with a picture of the eleven-year-old flying a red, white and blue kite which was printed in the *Florida Today* newspaper. Schwab, who had just been released from prison for molesting two young boys, saw the photo and determined that Junny was the boy that he wanted for himself.

Schwab first telephoned Junny under the pretense that he was a newspaper reporter who wanted to do another article on the young boy. "When he came to our door, he presented himself as a clean-cut young man, well-dressed, and driving a brand new Firebird with a t-top," Vicki says. "He didn't look like someone who had just gotten out of prison. He looked like a successful journalist. Of course, my son was in love with the car. He (Schwab) knew what was going to lure little boys. Schwab learned during that interview with Junny that he was really into surfing and was part of a Christian surfing group and had won several trophies."

After that first meeting in which Schwab wore a Florida Today badge to gain credibility, Schwab wrote the Rios-Martinez family an uplifting, encouraging letter about how good it was to meet them. At no time did Schwab work for the Florida Today newspaper or a surfing magazine as he said he did. It was all a lie.

Because of Junny's ardent interest in surfing, Schwab changed his tactics and told the Rios-Martinezes that he was now writing for a surfing magazine. He claimed that he would help the young boy do a resume and that he needed photos of him so he could gain a sponsorship for surfing. Schwab even went so far as to fake a sponsorship contract.

"Junny was so excited," Vicki says. "He was walking on Cloud Nine. However, my husband and I had our intuition firing off everywhere. At one time, I walked into the bedroom and my husband was getting out a gun. I said, 'What are you doing?' Junny's father was going to confront this man who claimed to be a reporter and make him tell them what he was really up to.'"

"My husband wanted to know who this man really was, who his father and mother were and what he wanted with our son," Vicki says. "Vicki calmed her husband down and had Schwab write down his name and address and other pertinent personal information.

Vicki and her husband tried to verify that Schwab really was a reporter for Florida Today, with no success. So they contacted a friend and had them run a background check on the name Schwab had given, which was Mark Dean. Because the name was incomplete, without Schwab's real last name, nothing came up.

As Schwab pursued his plan of isolating Junny from his family, Vicki and her husband said 'No' whenever Schwab asked to take Junny somewhere alone. There were many different times that, under the pretense of being a Florida Today writer, Schwab asked to take Junny out of school so he could take him to get his photo taken for the article that he was going to write. Vicki kept offering to go with them and, because of that, Schwab would then give an excuse and cancel the appointment.

"Schwab was way ahead of us," Vicki says. Over a three-week period, he brought Junny a (fake) contract to sign, tee shirts, and gift certificates. In prison he was taught to use computers so was able to devise the fake contract. He even had a phony schedule and expense account document that he said had to be signed. Throughout the charade, he kept trying to get permission from Junny's parents to take the child to Daytona to meet the fake sponsors.

What the Rios-Martinez family did not know was that recently, in a surfing magazine, there had been an article on the process of how to get a sponsorship. Schwab followed that article and based his plan on that.

"One of the last times he asked to get Junny was

for the weekend," Vicki says. Schwab pressured Vicki for permission to take Junny that weekend to meet his sponsor and Vicki said that they would work it out. He was supposed to pick Junny up and when Vicki said she wanted to go with them, Schwab canceled the appointment.

That fateful Thursday that Junny was kidnapped, Schwab called Junny's school, pretended to be the boy's father, and asked the school to tell Junny not to take the bus but instead to meet him at the ball-field. The message was given to Junny and he went to the park supposedly to meet his father.

Witnesses testified that at the park, a tall young man was seen with Junny. "Around that time, there were three phone calls made at the park to my home," Vicki says. "We don't know if that was Junny calling to ask permission to leave with him or if he (Schwab) was faking it saying he was calling and getting permission. Neither Junny's father nor I were here. We were at work.

The way that Schwab usually molested the children was with a knife at their throat. He would then make them take off one shoe, then one sock, then the next shoe, then the sock until he humiliated them into nakedness. That was to overpower them and then he took advantage of them."

Junny resisted Schwab's efforts to make him remove his clothes. The Rios-Martinez's know this because all of Junny's clothes were cut off of him. From the way it was done, it is believed that Schwab bound him first.

"The reason that Junny is dead," Vicki says, "Is

because if Mark Schwab violated his 15 years parole, he would go back to prison for his original sentence which was two life sentences. He knew that since Junny didn't cooperate, he had to eliminate the witness. That's why Junny is dead."

"Junny was supposed to be at home and then go to a ball game that night," Vicki says. "When Jeremy (Junny's brother) got off of the bus and saw that Junny wasn't there (at home), we just assumed that he was with his friends."

The family was concerned that Junny was not at home and made attempts to find him all over the neighborhood, friend's homes and at a fort the children had built. When Vicki finished at her job and went to the ball-field to watch Junny's ballgame, Vicki realized that her son wasn't there. She ran over to her husband and asked, "Where is Junny?" When they realized their son was missing, Vicki drove home figuring that he was probably at home by now. No one was there.

Vicki telephoned all his friends and made a time-line of where Junny had been all day and when he was last seen. She telephoned the school and learned the news that Junny's father had supposedly called the school and made arrangements to meet his son at the ball-field. During Vicki's conversation with the school, Junny's father walked in the door from the ballgame and Vicki asked him if he had called the school and made arrangements to meet Junny.

"I asked him if he found Junny and he said 'No.' Then I asked him if he called the school to meet Junny at the ball-field and he said, 'No. You call Mark's mother.

He has my son.' So, I called Mark Schwab's mother."

"When I called Schwab's mother, she lied to me and told me that Schwab was in Hawaii with Kelly Slater (a famous surfer) for the next two weeks," Vicki said. "I told her that my son was missing."

Vicki telephoned the police and asked them to get a photo of Schwab from his mother. "She did not co-operate with the police because she wanted to protect her son," Vicki says. "She may have been able to stop what was happening had she cooperated. We may have found him that night."

Junny was not found that night (Thursday) and was missing throughout the weekend until Tuesday. "They were the longest days of my life," Vicki says.

Schwab was finally located on Sunday in Ohio. The police told the Rios-Martinez family they had him in custody and to hope for the best about their son but to expect the worst.

"I can tell you that I had a media circus here (at home) for the entire time," Vicki says. "It was totally out of control because the media was here and friends and family and people we didn't even know were coming to our house and waiting for information. Nobody was in control. We were in no condition to be in charge."

The house was overrun with people going in and out, using their facililties. So much so, that the bath-room plumbing, and air conditioning in their home broke down.

"It is like all of a sudden you are part of a drama and you are swept into it. You don't even know how to play the role. It's like being in a pinball machine. I didn't want them here but they all wanted to help. They helped in the search for Junny, got fliers, and it was like a hub of communication."

On Sunday morning, Vicki's best friend arrived and helped gain order out of the chaos. "She totally took control and got everybody out of the house so we had a little peace," Vicki says. A table was placed outside for people to drop off food or sign a list documenting that they had been there.

While all that was going on, Schwab was brought back to Florida from Ohio and taken to different places where he claimed to have put Junny's body. Eventually, Schwab led the police to Canaveral Grove where he had placed a footlocker with Junny's body inside. Because the boy was too big for the container, a cord was wrapped around it to keep the lid down.

It was late in the evening on Tuesday, after a long day of searching by the family and friends, that the family got the news that an FBI agent was coming to talk with them about Junny. They gathered as a group at the door, awaiting the news of Junny's fate.

How did Vicki respond upon hearing what had happened to their son? "We said some prayers and as we waited they (friends and family) were all holding me up," Vicki says. "When he (the FBI agent) walked up to the door and he dropped his eyes, I collapsed. I didn't cry at first. I was in a total place that was total grace. I was being protected. It was like my body was there and I was outside my body, watching what was going on."

Later, after some of the people left the Rios-Martinez home, Vicki experienced a change. "I came back into my body," Vicki says. "It was very, very strange. This noise of a moan, I don't even know how to describe it, came up from my gut and it was between a moan and a scream. When I heard it, I didn't even realize it was me. I now know it is called a primal cry." Vicki's husband got off the couch and went running to comfort his wife. "He held onto me and I totally beat his back. It was unreal. I never experienced anything like that."

After things calmed down, Vicki was unable to go back to work. "I hid in the house," she says. "I couldn't stop crying. I couldn't be a professional."

How did the grief unfold for Vicki? "My husband just wrapped me up in his arms and took care of me as if I was a newborn baby. He did everything for me," Vicki says. "If I wanted to stay in bed all day, he cooked the meals, got the kids off to school and did everything for me as if I were an invalid."

"It was even difficult to go grocery shopping," Vicki said. "If I saw his favorite cereal, I'd just start crying. I had such a difficult time. I struggled with suicide daily."

"During the first year, there is grace to get you through it. You know it is there. It is like all the angels coming on a cloud. You know it's there. You can touch it. By the second year, the grace isn't there and you can feel it. Each first you went through the first time is even more emotional the second year. Most people aren't aware it is like that. One person said to me, 'It's been a year. Aren't you over it yet?' That didn't help.'"

Vicki's anger over what happened gave her the strength to help other people through working with

politicians on changing laws regarding child molesters. "We got the Junny Bill passed where they take the
gain time away from child molesters. The Predators Act
passed where we got public notification. Something very
good came out of this tragedy. As I started doing things
to help other people, that helped me the most," Vicki
says. "I started even going so far as telling people the
story to help people understand how the justice system
works. And that it is a great justice system if you are a
criminal because it is a 'criminal justice system.' I believe there is no justice for the victim."

Vicki found that the justice system and all that they
went through, fueled her anger. She was able to find
a therapist to help her deal with that and her suicidal
tendencies and was with him for about a year.

The denial part of Vicki's grieving was related to
the badly-decomposed condition of Junny's body when
it was found. It had been in the footlocker and because it didn't fit, there was a three-inch gap open to
the weather and bugs. While the footlocker was out
in the weather, it had rained every single night. "The
April showers that we had rained every single night,"
Vicki said. "And then the sun came out and just baked
it all day long." Because of the deterioration, they were
refused the opportunity to identify the body.

Denial was part of her grief. "I just know that, for
the first three months, I waited outside for him to come
home," Vicki says. "It felt like he was gone on a trip
like a field trip, or he went on a camping trip. He was
just gonna be riding his bike and come down the street.
My mind would not accept that he was not here. I knew

he was gone. I knew the dirty details, but my mind just could not accept it and I kept trying to tell them that I didn't get closure. There was no open casket. There was no body in a baseball uniform. He can't be dead. I didn't see him."

After about three months, Vicki was finally able to see the autopsy pictures. She knew she would have to identify certain pictures in court and she wanted to see them ahead of time. That was helpful for her acceptance of Junny's death. "You don't understand," Vicki said to her husband and others. "I can't accept it. I need to see it. I can accept the truth. Don't hide it from me." Seeing the pictures helped her get through the denial part of her grief.

Was there anything that made Vicki feel better through the process? "The biggest thing that eventually helped me, and it didn't happen until a year afterwards. They had sent a tree over from Rockledge Gardens for us to plant. The tree was planted in the side yard. I used to go out there and hug that tree. It had been planted for him in his memory and we almost lost it in a hurricane. I used to go out there and hug the tree and cry."

Vicki remembers the scores of plants that she received from others during her ordeal. Many were given away to friends and family and without a 'green thumb,' Vicki worried about the last plant that remained in her home. "I thought, 'when I kill that, he's really gonna be gone,'" Vicki says. "He (Junny) said to me, 'Mom. What do you want? A green thumb? So be it.' So now I have a green thumb. From that time on, gardening became my healing and it's taught me things."

Does Vicki remember anything that she was doing that made her feel worse? "Not necessarily anything that I did that made me worse," Vicki says. "My husband was extremely angry and much more angry than me because he was angry at God. And he was angry at anything and everybody. I was able to say, 'God didn't do this, Mark Schwab did this. I'm not mad at God.'"

Junny, Sr. wondered why God didn't step in and keep it from happening. "My husband's anger was unimaginable. There's no words for it. And I don't know how to explain that, when you are hurting to the core, the person that you love the most is taking their hurt out on you. It just makes life not even worth living. I finally got to the point that I realized that I was really close to taking my life, that I finally had to step in and tell him, 'I love you. I love you so much but I can't live like this. You come in and you take your anger out on me and I'm already hurt. All it does is make me want to take my own life. And for my own protection, I have to leave you.' I think my husband realized that he was not only going to have lost what he had lost, but he was going to lose the rest. It made him take a turn and realize that he couldn't take his anger out on me any longer and it made him change. That's the only thing I can think of that made me feel worse. The anger. The taking the anger out on each other."

Were there things people said or did that helped Vicki? "No words bring comfort in something like that," Vicki says. "Just holding you and the hugs help —more of the passing from soul to soul. You don't need words for that. To be honest with you, there were many customers that I lost because they couldn't face me. Then I would have other people who would come up just to say something and when they opened their mouth, nothing would come out. Then they would fall into tears and not even be able to talk. I ended up doing more comforting to other people than they did for me."

Did people say things that didn't help? "I just remember there was a class reunion that we went to, out on the beach," Vicki said. "A guy came up and he said he was so sorry and he just couldn't believe it and he was a father with a child the same age. He said he could not even imagine what we had been through. He finally just blurted out, 'I'm so glad that it happened to you and not to me because I couldn't have handled it.' When we turned around and left, my husband said, 'Was this supposed to comfort me?' Then, of course, there was the comment by the person who said, 'It's been a year, aren't you over it yet?' "

What role did Vicki's faith play in the grieving process? "I never, never gave up on my faith. My faith started years ago. I believe I came into the world already knowing Jesus. I know I sought out religion as a child and my mother let me go to church with anybody I wanted to. I went to Catholic, Jewish, Jehovah Witness, and others. So, I was able to seek Him out on my own."

Vicki talks about the discussions with Junny that she has now, even though he has passed over. "I started speaking to my son (Junny) three days after he was missing," Vicki says. "I didn't really tell anybody for the longest time, not even my husband, because I was afraid that, along with the suicide thoughts and talking to the spirits, that they would lock me up somewhere. But he (Junny) really explained to me so much more than I learned in church. He explained how things work and why things happened the way they did so I was much more willing to accept what had happened and to find a way to make it better and make a difference for other people. And he came for a purpose and the purpose was to bring child abuse to the fore-front. Because, for so many years, it was hidden behind closed doors and it's denied. And people don't talk about it. This case was in the fore-front. He told me, 'Mom, you knew this was going to happen. You chose to be my mother.'

I didn't lose my faith. My faith is what got me through those years. I needed to move away from the negativity and to create a beautiful environment that would make me want to live again."

How does Vicki cope now on a daily basis? "I learned that every moment is a gift and each day is a gift. And I just take it one day at a time, one moment at a time, one emotion at a time. I don't berate myself if a song comes on and it makes me think of him and I just sit there with tears rolling down my face. I allow the emotion to completely manifest itself and then I let it go."

How was grieving for their child Junny different from grieving for anyone else in Vicki's life? "Of course, there's the suddenness and the shock of it, and the horrible tragedy part of it where your mind wanders off into wondering what happened in that room. I try to stay away from there. When my mind goes there, I try and just lasso it and pull it back. It doesn't matter. I don't need to know all the gory details."

Vicki found that in grieving for her child, investigating the details was something she did more than for other family members who passed. "When my father died, I was right there and was able to say goodbye. It was different."

Does Vicki have any regrets about how she dealt with her grief about Junny?

"No. I realize now that grief is really a gift turned inside out and we don't know that going into it."

There were many things that Vicki learned that she would like the readers to know. "Junny and I were extremely close. We had an excellent relationship. There was never any doubt between us that we loved each other. And the biggest thing that I learned was that even after his physical body was gone, that same relationship was still there. We talk daily and I journal to him daily, and when I would get into my real, real bad grieving times, I wouldn't be able to hear him. And I would realize, 'I lost him. Now I lost him again.' And then, I would come back up and have some good days and my frequency and my vibration would be higher. And then he would come right in and speak to me and I could hear him. But then maybe something would happen and (my husband) would come in and scream and yell at me and hurt me emotionally with his anger and I would go back down into the depths of depression and I wouldn't be able to hear him (Junny).

I want to say that the thing that I learned the most is that you have a direct connection to heaven when you've lost someone to the other side. It's a direct connection. You didn't really lose them. You did not lose them at all. They're still right there. You can feel their presence.

For the first year, my phone rang every single night at about the same time and every time we would get up to answer it, nobody would be there. I did the star 69 and it would show that nobody was there. That was his (Junny's) way of trying to contact us to let us know that he was there with us. There were so many ways that he would try to make contact with me long before I learned how to stay at the highest frequency in order to stay in communication.

One Thanksgiving Day, my entire stereo system came on by itself. It takes three buttons to turn that on. I realize that every time he had a way of letting us know he was here. So, I ended up looking for the joy and for the gems out of the grief instead of staying in the depression.

I have a connection on the other side. I want to tell you it is one of the neatest things ever when you know that there is someone on the other side. And you know that they are out of pain. And it makes handling the grief so much better. When you put yourself in a higher vibration and you can hear them talk to you, it makes it so much more peaceful for you to be able to deal with such tragedy."

Postscript

Mark Dean Schwab was convicted of kidnapping, sexual battery of a child and first-degree murder of 11-year-old Junny in 1991. On Tuesday, July 1, 2008, Schwab was executed for his crimes by the state of Florida at Florida State Prison in Railford. His execution came 17 long years after his heinous acts. Junny's parents witnessed the execution which brought them the necessary closure and peace they deserved and needed for these terrible crimes against their son and family. Before the Rios-Martinez family was brought into the viewing room to watch the execution, Schwab was medicated, strapped down and covered with sheets which obscured everything but his head.

"While the execution brought us closure, it was a disappointment to all members of our family," Vicki says. "It was peaceful for Schwab, way too peaceful, in contrast to what he put Junny through. So, although we walked away with our closure, we were all left with a big disappointment. All we got to see was him receiving the final medication which executed him. Schwab even refused to look in our eyes and I was robbed of the opportunity of letting him know my feelings through my eyes looking into his."

In Loving Memory

The names, birthdays, date of passing,
and words that the parents of these beloved
children use to describe their child.

Marsha Simone Linton
Feb. 3, 1972 to August 15, 1993
Beautiful, fun, smart, sophisticated.

Randi Lee Allison
January 25, 1983 to July 15, 2007
Outspoken, fun-loving, giving, caring, full of life, feisty.

Jeannette "Tracy" Talbot Smith
September 25, 1959 to July 2, 1979
*Funny-funny-funny, great sense of humor, loved
children, excellent student, a nice kid.*

Makenzie Leigh Young
October 17, 1996 to Nov. 3, 2003
*Our little angel, outgoing, loud, sense of humor, sweet
disposition, loving.*

Kelly Dawn Heuer
July 31, 1968 to February 17, 1969
*Brilliant, perfect little angel, smiling, precious, happy,
never cried.*

Bonita "Sentis" Glenda Haywood
February 13, 1954 to Dec. 28, 2007
Generous, loving, intelligent, made strong friendships.

Frankie Everton Haywood
January 29, 1956 to Dec. 24, 2005
*Athletic, healthy, jovial, loved to laugh,
knowledgeable, trumpet player, loved his niece Shua,
so much fun.*

John Alexander Bishop
December 7, 1969 to May 14, 1972
*A good boy, a cuddly baby, sweet disposition, loved
music and books and loved to be read to.*

Mary "Chris" Szuba
October 26, 1956 to Nov. 29, 2007
*Fun to be with, great sense of humor, a doer, outgoing,
good parent, made things work, organized, a friend.*

Linda M. Hosburgh
June 8, 1957 to September 20, 1989
*Forgiving, dedicated to helping people, smart, caring,
lots of fun.*

David
July 31, 1957 to February 13, 1988
David had red hair and a beautiful singing voice. He was full of fun and nice to be around. He was concerned about how his mother would be after he was gone.

Howard Dewey Crandall II
August 3, 1947 to September/1968
Quirky sense of justice, looked out for others, wickedly funny, loyal, a genius, had a sweetness to him, had a tender heart.

Donnis "Donnie" Helms
August 4, 1971 to October 12, 2000
A man of integrity, a good boy, made everybody laugh, hard worker, very loving.

Steve Alan Brungard
May 1, 1953 to August 4, 1956
My angel, was special, sweet child, intelligent.

Valerie Susan Derr
February 6, 1963 to Feb 6, 1963
Precious newborn.

William "Billy" Robert Bonwell
September 15, 1980 to May 20, 2006
Free spirit, generous.

Christy Lee Young
August 22, 1977 to August 22, 1977
Precious newborn.

Lisa Garrod
February 1, 1963 to June 5, 2005
Loved nature, had a green thumb, happy, thankful for each day.

Baby Boy Zerick
February 16, 1948 to February 16, 1948
Precious newborn.

Timothy Dale Zerick
January 5, 1961 to January 5, 1961
Beautiful. Perfect in every way.

Jared Jim Hodgins
July 23, 1981 to April 29, 1998
A good kid, protector of his brother, peacekeeper, athletic, had magnetism, full of life.

Robert E. Best
September 21, 1953 to September 4, 2007
Special, A caring son, wonderful to his parents, good husband-father-grandfather, family man.

Dennis Richard McMahon III
September 4, 1954 to July 10, 1982
One who didn't have to study. Learned automatically and loved to learn.

Michael "Mike" Jerome McMahon
October 22, 1963 to November 27, 2004
Natural friend and leader of the military. They all loved him.

Andy Tant
August 8, 1980 to December 8, 1996
Had a great sense of humor, a servant's heart, very loyal.

W. Brandon Seidel
November 24, 1968 to June 20, 2008
Lots of fun, hard-worker, good dad, loving, had many talents and abilities.

Junny Rios-Martinez
May 6, 1979 to April 18, 1991
Full of life. Good at everything he did. He had a sensitivity far beyond his years. He enjoyed life and loved the outdoors. He was like a magnet in drawing others to him. Charismatic.

Resource Page

Helpful Contacts For Grieving Parents

GriefShare
P O Box 1739
Wake Forest, North Carolina 27588
1-800-395-5755, Ext. 246
www.griefshare.org

Centering Corporation
7230 Maple Street
Omaha, Nebraska 68134
866-218-0101
402-553-1200
Fax - 402-553-0507
www.centering.org
"North America's oldest and largest bereavement resource center."

The Compassionate Friends
Toll Free: 877-969-0010
Phone: 630-990-0010
Fax: 630-990-0246
www.compassionatefriends.org
"Supporting Family After a Child Dies. A Self-Help Bereavement Organization."

The Dougy Center
"The National Center For Grieving Children and Families"
   P O Box 86852
   Portland, OR 97286
   Phone: 503-775-5683
   Toll Free: 866-775-5683
   Fax: 503-777-3097
   Email: help@dougy.org
   www.dougy.org

Alive Alone
"For Parents whose only child/all children have died"
   1112 Champaign Drive
   Van Wert, OH 45891
   www.alivealone.org
   Email: alivalon@bright.net

UNITE, Inc.
"Grief Support After Miscarriage, Stillbirth and Infant Death"
   P O Box 65
   Drexel Hill, PA 19026
   or
   UNITE, Inc. Grief Support
   c/o Jeanes Hospital
   7600 Central Avenue
   Philadelphia, PA 19111-2499
   Phone: (215) 728-3777
   Toll Free: 888-48-6483
   Email: administrator@unitegriefsupport.org
   www.unitegriefsupport.org

Center of Loss in Multiple Births   (CLIMB, Inc.)
"A quarterly newsletter for parents of multiple birth death"
c/o Jean Kollantai
P O Box 91377
Anchorage, AK 99509
Phone: (907) 222-5321
newsletter@climb-support.org
www.climb-support.org

Parents of Murdered Children
"Provides self-help groups to support people who are suffering through the violent death of someone close."
100 E. 8th St., B-41
Cincinnati, OH 45202
Phone: (513) 721-5683
Toll Free: (888) 818-POMC
Fax: (513) 345-4489
natlpomc@aol.com
www.pomc.com

GROWW
Grief Recovery For All Bereaved
Anne D'Ambrosio, Executive Director
11877 Douglas Road
#102-PMB101
Alpharetta, GA 30005
http://www.groww.org/

Bereaved Parents of the USA
P O Box 95
Park Forest, IL 60466
Phone: (708) 748-7672
Fax: (708) 748-9184
president@bereavedparentsusa.org

Bibliography

Capter One:

1. "The Autobiography of Mark Twain", arranged and edited by Charles Neider, Harper & Brothers, New York, 1959.

2. "Lincoln, An Illustrated Biography", Philip B. Kunhardt, Jr., Philip B. Kunhardt, III, Peter W. Kunhardt, Alfred A. Knopf, New York.